HISTORICAL GROUND

Historical Ground investigates how contemporary landscape architecture invokes and displays the history of a site. In the light of modernism's neglect of history, these essays by John Dixon Hunt explore how, in fact, designers do attach importance to how a location manifests its past.

The process involves, on the one hand, registering how geography, topography and climate determine design and, on the other, how history discovered or even created for a site can structure its design and its reception. History can be evident, exploited, invented or feigned – it can be original or a new history which becomes part of how we view a place.

Landscapes discussed in this book come from across Europe and the United States, highlighting the work of designers who have drawn from site history in their design, or have purposefully created their own historical account of the location. The author explores not just the historical past, but how new ground can be given a life and a future.

John Dixon Hunt is Emeritus Professor of the History and Theory of Landscape at the University of Pennsylvania. He is the author of more than a dozen books and edits the Taylor & Francis journal *Studies in the History of Gardens & Designed Landscapes* and is the series editor of the Penn Studies in Landscape Architecture.

HISTORICAL GROUND

The role of history in contemporary landscape architecture

John Dixon Hunt

LONDON AND NEW YORK

First published 2014
by Routledge
2 Park Square, Milton Park, Abingdon, Oxon OX14 4RN

and by Routledge
711 Third Avenue, New York, NY 10017

Routledge is an imprint of the Taylor & Francis Group, an informa business

© 2014 John Dixon Hunt

The right of John Dixon Hunt to be identified as author of this work has been asserted by him in accordance with sections 77 and 78 of the Copyright, Designs and Patents Act 1988.

Every effort has been made to contact and acknowledge copyright owners. If any material has been included without permission, the publishers offer their apologies. The publishers would be pleased to have any errors or omissions brought to their attention so that corrections may be published at a later printing.

All rights reserved. No part of this book may be reprinted or reproduced or utilised in any form or by any electronic, mechanical, or other means, now known or hereafter invented, including photocopying and recording, or in any information storage or retrieval system, without permission in writing from the publishers.

Trademark notice: Product or corporate names may be trademarks or registered trademarks, and are used only for identification and explanation without intent to infringe.

British Library Cataloguing in Publication Data
A catalogue record for this book is available from the British Library

Library of Congress Cataloging in Publication Data
Hunt, John Dixon.
Historical ground : the role of history in contemporary landscape architecture / John Dixon Hunt.
pages cm
Includes bibliographical references and index.
1. Landscape architecture. 2. Landscape design. I. Title.
SB476.H86 2014
712—dc23
2013024631

ISBN: 978-0-415-81412-6 (hbk)
ISBN: 978-0-415-81413-3 (pbk)

Typeset in Bembo
by FiSH Books Ltd, Enfield

Printed and bound in Great Britain by
TJ International Ltd, Padstow, Cornwall

For
David Leatherbarrow

CONTENTS

List of illustrations	*ix*
Preface	*xiii*

1	Preliminary orientations	1
2	History as geology, topography and weather	15
	Geology 17	
	Topography 27	
	Weather 35	
3	Examples of history in earlier landscape architecture: Renaissance Rome, Désert de Retz, Les Buttes Chaumont	45
4	Five Parisian sites: a scale of contemporary interventions and inventions	53
5	History found and exploited in a specific place	63
	Memorials 63	
	Drosscapes and others 78	
	Remembrance of things past 86	
	Historical reminiscences of plants, planting and garden forms 95	
6	History "invented" for a site today	106
	A middle ground 107	
	True invention and a "most feigning" history 116	
	Avant gardeners 132	

viii Contents

7 Land art, garden festivals and historical ground   138

8 Afterword/Afterlife   156

Select bibliogaphy   *161*
Index   *163*

LIST OF ILLUSTRATIONS

1.1	Lawrence Halprin, The FDR Memorial, Washington, DC, using quotations from FDR as part of the narrative	4
1.2	Houghton, Norfolk, UK. A Victorian garden beneath the modern lawn in a dry summer	7
1.3	Het Loo, Apeldoorn, The Netherlands	7
2.1	The Great Avenue, Castle Howard, Yorkshire, UK	18
2.2	Paolo Bürgi, The Geological Observatory, Cardada, Switzerland	19
2.3	Luis Baragán, El Pedregal (The Rocky Place) Mexico City	21
2.4	A distant view of the city of Nîmes, France, from one of the Belvederes at the rest area, with a maquette of the Roman Tour Magne in the city, designed by Bernard Lassus	23
2.5	The Quarries at the Crazannes rest area, France	24
2.6	Michael van Valkenburgh, Teardrop Park, New York	25
2.7	PROAP, Lagos City Park, Portugal, 2003–2009: relation between the Castle and the park	31
2.8	PROAP, Masterplan for the Promenade de l'Indépendance, Algiers, 2007: access to the Monument	32
2.9	Paolo Bürgi, re-envisaging the fields with new ploughing and sowing in the German Ruhr	34
2.10	George Hargreaves, Guadalupe River Park, San Jose, CA	35
2.11	Günther Vogt, The Weather Garden, Park Hyatt Hotel, Zürich	38
2.12	Michael Van Valkenburgh, Mill Race Park, Columbus, IN	40
2.13	PROAP, Barcelos Fluvial Park, Portugal, 2004–2009: topographical elements	41
2.14	Olin Studio, stormwater management, M.I.T. Stata Centre	42
2.15	Lawrence Halprin, "Sea Ranch Ecoscore"	44
3.1	Palatine Hill, Rome	46

x List of illustrations

3.2	G.B. Falda engraving of the gardens on the Palatine Hill, 1670s	47
3.3	Désert de Retz, near Chambourcy, France. (a) Chinese House (demolished), engraving from late 18th century, and (b) the "Ruined Column", with theatre fragment in the foreground	49
3.4	Parc des Buttes Chaumont, Paris, France. (a) The suspension bridge by Eiffel, and (b) one of the many fences cast in concrete in imitation of tree trunks	51
4.1	Parc André Citroën, Paris. Plan of the park and inset of the bust of Monsieur Citroën	54
4.2	Parc Bercy, Paris. Plan of the site	56
4.3	Parc (formerly Jardin) Diderot, La Défense, Paris	57
4.4	Jardin Atlantique, Gare Montparnasse, Paris. The "boardwalk" and the "waves"	58
4.5	Jardin Atlantique, Gare Montparnasse, Paris. The "caves" in the "cliff"	59
4.6	Les Jardins d'Eole, Paris	61
5.1	The memorial by Wiktor Tolkin at Majdanek, Poland	66
5.2	The 9/11 Memorial, New York	68
5.3	Invalidenplatz, Berlin, Germany	70
5.4	PROAP, four details of the proposed memorial parkland dedicated to Memory and Oblivion in Flanders Fields, Belgium	73
5.5	Kathryn Gustafson and Neil Porter, plan for the Garden of Forgiveness (Hadiqat As-Samah), Beirut	75
5.6	Exchange Square, Manchester, UK	76
5.7	Philadelphia Municipal Pier II, designed by Field Operations	80
5.8	Brooklyn Bridge Park, New York City	81
5.9	Peter Latz + Partner, gardens in the Duisburg-Nord Landscape Park, Germany	83
5.10	Peter Latz + Partner, steel columns in the Parc Dora, Turin, Italy	85
5.11	Adriaan Geuze, "Horizon Project", with huge inflatable cows in a redolent Dutch landscape	88
5.12	Bernard Lassus, Le Jardin des Retours, Rochefort sur Mer, France, with the Corderie Royale in the background, and the ramp into the garden from the upper civic parkland marked by lines of Virginia Liriodendron	89
5.13	The riverside walks at Green Bay, Wisconsin	90
5.14	João Gomes da Silva, "Unseen Gardens", Lisbon, Portugal	91
5.15	Laurie Olin, drawing for the Wexner Center, The Ohio State University, Columbus, OH	100
5.16	Dan Kiley, Fountain Place, Dallas, Texas	101
5.17	The flooded quarry in the Shanghai Botanical Gardens	103
5.18	Catherine Mosbach, the Botanical Garden at Bordeaux, France	104
6.1	Garden games of Bernard Lassus, Chateau de Barbirey-sur-Ouche, Burgundy, France	107

List of illustrations **xi**

6.2	Georges Descombes, the Chanzeli on the the Swiss Path, Lake Uri, Switzerland	109
6.3	George Hargreaves, the folded ridges of the Clinton Presidential Center, Little Rock, Arkansas	111
6.4	George Hargreaves, Louisville Riverfont Park, Kentucky	113
6.5	Parque del Clot, Barcelona, Spain	113
6.6	Bernard Lassus, the reception "garden" at COLAS HQ, Paris	115
6.7	The Garden of Cosmic Speculation, Portrack House, near Dumfries in South West Scotland: The Jumping Bridge	118
6.8	The Garden of Cosmic Speculation, Portrack House, near Dumfries in South West Scotland. The Soliton Waves gate	119
6.9	The Garden of Cosmic Speculation, Portrack House, near Dumfries in South West Scotland. The Universe Cascade	121
6.10	Little Sparta, Dunsyre near Edinburgh, Scotland. Ian Hamilton Finlay, steel cut-out figures after Bernini's Apollo and Daphne	122
6.11	Ian Hamilton Finlay, with Alexandre Chemetoff, Sue Finlay and Nicholas Sloan, an opening of "Le Jardin révolutionnaire", Hôtel des Menus Plaisirs, Versailles, 1988	124
6.12	Le Jardin de la Noria, near Uzès, Provence, France	127
6.13	Le Jardin de l'Alchimiste, Provence, France	128
6.14	Ian Hamilton Finlay, stones carved with words of the French historian Michelet, Fleur de l'Air, Provence, France	129
6.15	Martha Schwartz, frogs in a pool at a redundant shopping centre, Atlanta, Georgia	131
6.16	Paolo Bürgi, private garden, Padua, Italy. The end of the Percorso fra I Bambù, 1999	135
6.17	Paolo Bürgi, Tree "follies" – perspective, and false perspective – at the Organizzazione Sociopsichiatria Cantonale, Mendrisio, Ticino, Switzerland, 1986–89	136
7.1	Michael Heizer, Double Negative, Nevada Desert, near Overton, NV	139
7.2	Magdalena Jetelová, Big Chair, 1985–86, Forest of Dean, Gloucestershire, UK	142
7.3	The Scent Garden, by the University of Toronto, Xi'an International Horticultural Exposition, China, 2011	144
7.4	(a and b) Karl Kullmann, axonometric diagrams of the Master's Gardens and the University Gardens at the Xi'an International Horticultural Exposition, China, 2011	145
7.5	Philippe Coignet and David Serero, "Modulations", project for les Jardins de Métis in 2005	148
7.6	Kathryn Gustafson and Neil Porter, plan for their installation, "Towards Paradise", at the Venice Biennale, 2003	150
7.7	David Meyer and Ramsey Silberberg "Limelight", Westonbirt Garden Festival 2003	151
7.8	Ken Smith, Santa Fe Railyard Park, New Mexico	154

xii List of illustrations

7.9 Ken Smith, Martha Schwartz and David Meyer, Yorkville Park,
Toronto 154

Afterword/Afterlife.1 Lawrence Halprin's Heritage Park in Fort Worth,
Texas 160

PREFACE

This is a book about the role of history in the making of, and response to, contemporary landscape architecture. It emerges from some of my previous considerations of meaning in landscape architecture more generally and, recently, from the chance to explore this particular topic with students of landscape architects. Yet it approaches the larger theme of meaning in somewhat different ways: it asks how the history of a particular site may be invoked and used in a new intervention. And it asks that question, firstly, because too much modernist landscape architecture seemed to turn its back on the past and, secondly, because much contemporary landscape architecture is uninterested in locality – especially those great and good landscape architects who fly around the world to create new places where they really know little about the site or even the history of the country where it is to be made. If they do show such an interest, it is likely to be superficial, the work of fancy not imagination (to use Coleridge's famous distinction that I shall take up in Chapter 4). I have seen too many students in studios fly off for a week of "site visits" to a country where they do not speak the language and have an utterly brief grasp of the local culture and then come home to propose a design: it's good training in some respects, but it cultivates a habit that sees any place anywhere as a suitable place to dump a design, however skilful.

This small book arose, first, out of an invitation to talk at a symposium at the University of Venice on history and landscape (subsequently published as *Storia* [i.e., history] *e Paessagio* in 2013); this talk was later augmented for a public lecture at Dumbarton Oaks, and then revisited for a presentation on "Topography" at a university in Nanjing, China (the latter was published in *Architectural Studies*, no.2, issue on "Topography & Mental Space" ed. Mark Cousins *et al.*, China Architecture & Building Press, 2012). It also was a topic taken up in a graduate seminar at the University of Pennsylvania in 2010, and has now been finalized during the teaching of a seminar at Penn State University in Spring 2013, where the final draft of these

xiv Preface

essays was completed. From all those encounters, I have derived many suggestions and responses from members of those audiences, from colleagues at Penn State and from students there: I have been greatly helped by two research assistants, Nathan Gandrud and Elissa Jane Ferguson.

The book is essentially a collection of essays – since it is not intended as a complete survey of the idea, but rather to suggest ways in which the theme may be taken up by both practitioners and users for further exploration and illustration. It starts with two essays setting out some preliminary issues about the possible role of the historian, and then how geology, topography and weather impact the process of making the historical site. Then come two shorter chapters: first, on three examples of historical representations from the past; second, a discussion of five Parisian contemporary sites; both the early examples and the contemporary ones in Paris provide a useful scale of reference for the larger topic. After that come two long chapters that focus on the two dominant themes of the book – how history is manifested in places that provide designers with the material for that reference, and then how history could be fabricated, manufactured or "feigned" for sites and how such invention works. Finally, it seemed worth looking at how land art plays a role in registering the history of place, but also how little land art actually impacted what can legitimately be termed landscape architecture; that provided a final sequence on the recent flurry of garden festivals and exhibitions and their relevance to historical ground.

I have relied, as my notes and captions acknowledge, on a large resource of publications, both issued by landscape firms themselves or by publishers wishing to record a single designer or a range of examples. A list of the most-cited volumes is appended at the end of the book. I have benefitted hugely from this resource, and my own observations draw both on these volumes and what their texts and images suggest to me as well as on my own visits to these sites. I have also taken suggestions for historical (or sometimes non-historical) projects from students, who can be suspicious of too much historical awareness in contemporary work and, above all, in a landscape historian like me.

I thank most warmly the friends, colleagues and designers who have helped me to obtain illustrations for the text: Paolo Bürgi, Philippe Coignet, Jennifer Current, Georges Descombes, Stuart Echols, Adriaan Geuze, George Hargreaves, Charles Jencks, Karl Kullmann, Bernard Lassus, Peter Latz, David Meyer, João Nunes, Laurie Olin, Neil Porter, Chris Reed, Martha Schwartz, Gideon Fink Shapiro, João Gomes da Silva, Michael Van Valkenburgh, Günther Vogt, Peter Walker, Udo Weilacher, Tom Williamson, and James E. Young.

1

PRELIMINARY ORIENTATIONS

"What would it mean for a culture to give up on its past?"

(Stephen Greenblatt)[1]

"There has never been a time when...a study of history provides so little instruction for our present day"

(Tony Blair)[2]

History is not the past. It is our knowledge of the past, more precisely our attending to some narrative of the past that was told then and is recalled for us now, or that we re-tell in some form today. It is also, these days, hard to think of places without some history that has been told either in the past (and maybe forgotten) or recounted now (so much for Tony Blair!). Some cultures, and some places, have a stronger inclination to live the past, nourishing its stories and the various ways in which they come alive for their inhabitants; others are much more focused on the present and, deliberately or not, decline to listen to those narratives that they consider merely nostalgia.

Landscape architecture, we might suppose, has no site these days that is without some historical ground. Few places are "empty" of history. Although when Robert Frost recited his poem "The Gift Outright" for the inauguration of President Kennedy, he choose to celebrate a myth of the visionary westward movement by new immigrants to North America, buoyed by the vision of a world where they could build, farm and garden in a landscape that was (Frost wrote) "unstoried, artless, unenhanced". Doubtless those new settlers wished to believe this; but the

---

1   Stephen Greenblatt, *New York Times Book Review*, 26 August, 2012.
2   Tony Blair addressing the American Congress on the eve of the Iraq war, cited by Nicholas Vincent in the *Times Literary Supplement*, 15 June 2012.

2 Preliminary orientations

idea that native Americans possessed no stories, were without arts or did not, in some fashion, enhance the lands where they dwelt, was sadly wrong. These days we live in a world that is hugely storied and enhanced – or at least one that has been messed up with the debris of the past we no longer want or need, even if it is "part of history". As a teenager I dreamed of climbing the as-yet un-scaled Mount Everest, but in the years after it was scaled (led incidentally by somebody called Hunt; no relation, but a happy stand-in), the mountain was under constant siege; its slopes are now eminently storied[3] and enhanced, regrettably, by the bodies of those who failed in their ascent as well as by the debris of oxygen bottles that fuelled their climbs.

Yet back in the early 18th century, if you were living in London, a city where rebuilding and expanding the urban land was insistent, you could still read in the poem *London* – which Samuel Johnson published in 1738 – a hope for virgin land somewhere else in the world:

> Has heaven reserv'd, in pity to the poor,
> No pathless waste, or undiscover'd shore;
> No secret island in the boundless main?
> No peaceful desart yet unclaim'd by Spain?

(lines 170–3)

Today there are very few, if any, pathless wastes or undiscovered shores. Many landscape architects seem – and I emphasize "seem" – to delight in tackling what they consider pathless wastes, some toxic or industrial wasteland, some derelict cityscape, to fashion it into some exciting and new social space, as if it had no history.

There is, of course, no obligation for landscape architects to celebrate historical ground. Indeed, as artists, they cherish the chance to make something new – a result of both their own artistic visions and their indebtedness to a modernism that declines to be interested in the past. Yet many designers whom I know spend a great deal of time understanding a site and its culture, including its historical events, before they embark on their own projects; sometimes their explorations of the original past can find expression in a new place. But it is often not their priority – for many reasons: their own lack of interest in the past as opposed something they can make that is new; their clients' concern to make a modern splash; a community committed, understandably, to seeing that its location responds to current needs. I suspect that there is a stronger impulse in Europe to respond to historical ground than in the United States.

But there is also the lack of both opportunity and a suitable vocabulary to find some means of making history visible. Landscape architects are not historians, and

---

3   The library is full now of these accounts: see especially Robert Macfarlane, *Mountains of the Mind* (New York: Pantheon Books, 2003) and Wade Davis, *Into the Silence: The Great War, Mallory and the conquest of Everest* (New York: Vintage Books, 2011).

even if they do some research on a site's history prior to redesigning it, they have probably little skill in articulating some aspect of the past. It is rare that they'd ask a *bone fide* historian to work for them, but even then they themselves have the obligation to find formal, palpable ways of making that history visible, which the historian is less capable of doing than (presumably) a landscape architect. Some practitioners do this, as we shall see, but often the history seeps, so to speak, from the site regardless of any formal decision by the designer. One seepage is that the past vocabulary of garden- and park-making makes itself felt unconsciously in the very forms and devices that are still used: we still rely on paths, viewpoints, grading of the earth and mounds, tunnelling, decoration with sculpture, and insertion of buildings; we shall see much of that in the following pages. However, some designers, as I shall also suggest, can "invent" a history for the place, a history that may have little or no reason for being there, but one that can take hold and infect visitors' imagination with a sense of something plausibly historical. I want to call these *fabricated histories*, as opposed to fractured ones (the real hints and possibilities that do emerge).

One of the issues for a landscape architect is that even if he or she *were* an accomplished historian, they are not physically present on the site that they design. They can write – retrospectively by subsequently recording their original intentions – that their work reflects, say, ancient Roman brickwork: on the architectural arches at the Robert F. Wagner Jr. Park in Battery Park, New York, Laurie Olin explained that "This was achieved through the use and material pointedly reminiscent of Flavian brickwork as seen in the ruins at Ostia Antica … and through the suggestion of an anthropomorphic transformation of the structures into a buried and deracinated head of a colossus gazing fixedly out into the harbour" towards the Statue of Liberty.[4] This is intriguing, yet it has little traction on the site itself; the historical details may work for the original designer, but – in the absence of a personal commentary and his or her ability to "point" out those ideas on the spot – they are meaningless; visitors have to make sense of what they see by themselves.

By contrast, a historian, writing, has control of his narrative; he or she can structure the argument, the tonal nuances, even the facts, by which the story can be told and insinuated. A film maker and a novelist have similar ways of directing our understanding of the tales they tell; they edit and nudge our reading of the narrative. Even a painter, though usually not a visible presence in the painting (there are interesting exceptions[5]), can so structure the scene, its characters and their action that we grasp how that particular history goes, or we know enough of the event (from its title, for example) to see how the artist has slanted or loaded the tale. For no history is wholly objective nor innocent, and the teller of the tale (the historian) plays a fundamental role in directing the narrative.

4   Laurie Olin, "What I do when I can do it: Representation in recent work", *Studies in the History of Gardens and Designed Landscapes,* 19 (1999), p.143.
5   The painting by Velázquez, *Las Meninas,* shows the painter confronting the unseen royal couple who are notionally behind the viewer.

4 Preliminary orientations

But the landscape architect has none of those possible roles. He or she can neither report objectively nor direct the telling of the tale. There are some exceptions. When Lawrence Halprin designed the FDR Memorial in Washington, DC, he followed the leads of previous monuments in that capital and used words, by which at least part of the history was readily made available (Figure 1.1). In addition, by laying out FDR's career in four rooms, to signal his four terms as president, Halprin could tell a story about his life, since the rooms were a sequence and the quoted words were, as always with words, sequential. (It is however, a touch awkward if visitors get into the fourth room first; but they can backtrack and start in the first). Halprin himself is not there, though presumably a park ranger can perform that story for him and his design; but Halprin's choice of quotations and his layout did articulate a history, even for those with only a slight recall of FDR's presidency. So the designer can act as narrator, and we can adjudicate that narrative for how it consorts with the history that we ourselves bring to such a memorial.

That narratives can be history is self-evident ("Once upon a time..."); but it is not always evident that the historical event is thereby made clear. In the case of Halprin's FDR Memorial, he narrates, dramatizes and images the presidential career, and from that we derive a sense of (or we tell ourselves about) FDR's career, its political history and its sequences in response to what we see and read. We shall

FIGURE 1.1 Lawrence Halprin, The FDR Memorial, Washington, DC, using quotations from FDR as part of the narrative.

frequently in the pages that follow encounter this slippage, a slipping from image into implied narrative and thence into a historical moment that is reified in that place. Man has always been *homo narrator*.[6] It must also be noted that narratives are themselves an inventive operation rather than a factual one. Where some narrative is not articulated – when for example we see some image of a far-away place,[7] or observe the autumn foliage – we may still derive a historical sense by the simple fact that we narrate it to each other or to ourselves. Part of a historical narrative may take the form of a recitation or rehearsal of associations that pertain to that event; those in their turn, though, call out for some reciprocal response by visitors. In this, both landscape narratives and associations are "performed", and performances require an audience.

But often designers will have neither words that help to tell a story nor a sequence by which a narrative might emerge. Many designers deplore the use of words or the use of inscriptions in their designs; nor do many gardens and landscapes have a specific route by which we can unravel a tale – we tend to do it retrospectively, putting the bits and pieces that we find while exploring together into a narrative constructed retrospectively.[8] And we may also find that gardens can invent a narrative for us, or we do it for them in responding to what we find there. In the film, *L'année dernière à Marienbad,* a man and a woman on a garden terrace discuss a statue nearby and what the site means. The man explains to the woman how the statue of the male figure is holding the woman back or somehow frustrating her. It is the character's personal fiction, of course, but it supposedly informs his understanding of the landscape and how the two of them see it and each other. But a little later in the film a rather boring figure starts to explain the "historical" meaning of the sculptural pair by saying that the male figure was actually that of Charles III, and the 'historian' then proceeds to explain its "true" history. Interestingly, though, as he begins to tell that story, the film, typically, trails off and leaves us without him finishing that "history"![9]

So it may be that the story envisaged by the designer, or something approximating to that original design, may be a wholly different tale from the one invented by a visitor according to how she or he responds to it. So, it is often possible that the "reception" of sites and landscapes has simply nothing to do with an "original" design; visitors now respond to whatever they find to say about it. This is highly problematical and indeed complex, and we have not really begun to grasp how to

---

6   Jay Gould, "So Near and So Far", *New York Review of Books* (20th October, 1994), p.26.
7   I am thinking here of the Jardin Atlantique (see Chapter Four) where an imagined place is "narrated" by a specific garden design and this supplies us with a narrative about a place that offers some history in our lives or in contemporary culture (the invention of the seaside). For the narrative of autumn leaves, see Chapter Two.
8   I have approached this topic in "Stourhead revisited and the pursuit of meaning in gardens", *Studies in the History of Gardens and Designed Landscapes,* 26/4 (2006).
9   In fact, for this incident Alain Resnais invented the statue, partly based on a figure in a Poussin painting: see Suzanne Liandrat-Guigues and Jean-Louis Leutrat, *Alain Resnais: Liaisons secrètes, accords vagabonds* (Cahiers du Cinéma, 2006), pp.223–4.

6 Preliminary orientations

confront this very complex matter of what I have called the "afterlife of gardens".[10] This afterlife is not, however, to be entirely rejected; for one thing, though we tend too easily to speak of and rely on "personal" stories, these are themselves often directed by a culture that shapes more than a single response. How we ourselves respond to a topography and its history is ultimately and importantly part of the site, whether it is invented or originates on the site.

Many modern designs are laid down, not on one particular historical ground, but on many layers. One metaphor is useful here: the palimpsest is a parchment that, once written on, can be scraped away, and a new text laid down on top of the old; the term is from the Greek, *palimpsestos*, meaning "scraped and reused". In many cases the new text has nothing to do with what it covers over. For example: in the 10th-century a scribe copied out several works by Archimedes (the scientist, mathematician and inventor from the 3rd century BC). Then on Easter Eve in April of 1229 a priest-scribe called Ioannes Myronas erased the Archimedes text and superimposed his own prayer book. Recently, however, experts working on the Archimedes Codex have been able to recover the Greek work beneath the Christian one.[11]

So how does this help us in thinking about gardens? Since a garden is not a parchment, but a physical space usually of some scope (certainly bigger than a piece of parchment) in which one design can be eliminated ("scraped" away, buried or lost) and another one superimposed upon it, it is three-dimensional in a way that a piece of parchment cannot be said to be. The garden or park can be either a complete fresh layer of garden or parkland, or (to keep our eyes more on landscape architecture than parchments) it can have different items from different earlier periods, and even different cultures, placed on it. The new layer can, of course, be imposed on something that was not a garden – a former street or thoroughfare, the remains of an old town, a disused and maybe toxic industrial plant. Sometimes, the earlier one, whatever it was, can be seen or glimpsed below the new one: occasionally in dry summers, the layout of an earlier garden can be detected beneath the present one (Figure 1.2).

Yet more often than not the new garden or park obliterates the old, which the visitor no longer sees. This was the case originally with the garden of the Paleis Het Loo at Apeldoorn in The Netherlands. In fact, Het Loo gardens are a double-layered palimpsest (Figure 1.3): a late 17th-century Dutch garden was covered over with an English-style pastoral landscape in the 19th century that completely buried the earlier design; but then in the 1980s the Dutch government decided to restore the first William and Mary garden. Using a combination of discovering some

---

10 See my book, *The Afterlife of Gardens* (London: Reaktion Books, 2004). The idea that any response is just or correct (*tot homines, quot sententiae* – as many ideas as there are people – in the Latin tag) is ultimately not very plausible.

11 See William Noel, Reviel Netz, Natalie Tchernetska, and Nigel Wilson, eds., *The Archimedes Palimpsest*, 2 vols (Cambridge, UK: Cambridge University Press, 2011) and see http://archimedespalimpsest.net/.

Preliminary orientations 7

FIGURE 1.2 Houghton, Norfolk, UK. A Victorian garden beneath the modern lawn in a dry summer. Photograph: Derek Edwards for Norfolk Landscape Archaeology, Norfolk County Council.

FIGURE 1.3 Het Loo, Apeldoorn, The Netherlands. In the background is the 17th-century restored garden in the 1980s, with remnants of a "pastoral" landscape from the 19th century, notably a tree and lawn, in the foreground.

8 Preliminary orientations

physical remains below the landscaped soil and then invoking a corpus of 17th-century engravings, the first garden was reconstructed. However in one area, partly so as not to destroy a tree that was beloved by Dutch people because the current Queen liked it, a bit of the English-style landscape was left, exposing, if you like, the 19th-century layer below the current, modern recreation of the 17th-century one. Furthermore, to the observant eye of a visitor, and certainly for the knowledgeable historian, certain bits and pieces of the original Dutch garden, the stone outlines of channels on the parterres, for example, were incorporated into the modern recreation, along with careful reconfigurations of fountains from detailed engravings at the time, all of which refer directly to the earliest garden. So at Het Loo we can understand three levels – the new, modern garden, a 19th-century fragment that signals a larger whole and, by implication, the original garden now restored or reinvented. And in a precise, archaeological sense, the earlier garden forms and items (fountains, cascades, even the "pastoral" tree, etc.) were used to recall that earlier historical ground.

For historians, like the teams that worked to restore the first Het Loo, there are obviously ways in which to access and maybe show off an earlier garden or site – drawings, old engravings, archaeology (though this may destroy part of the new to get down to the old), or sonar sounding. But generally if a new garden covers the old, the modern visitor – who is not a historian – has only the sight of what he *sees now*, which is likely to offer little sense of what was there before.

So another issue suggests itself: can we deliberately *make* a garden that can be *understood* as a palimpsest, as opposed to just covering up one that is deemed old-fashioned or maybe too expensive to maintain? How do we do that? These days, when so much space in the world is already pre-empted, we are likely to have to make new gardens on top of other things, and therefore it becomes interesting to ask how an earlier site could, or should, be made visible and how it can tell its tale. How are the earlier levels of a site to be "read"? Can we see them? Do we just "guess" at them?[12] Or simply read notices, guidebooks or digital displays that explain – indirectly – what was there but which we now cannot see?

One further idea of the palimpsest as parchment comes from Umberto Eco, and this is relevant to what I call a fabricated history. A palimpsest, its erasures and its newly inscribed narratives, are at the heart of his novel, *Baudolino*. The "hero" and narrator Baudolino has taught himself to write by practising on an ancient parchment from which he has scraped earlier writings: "I have scraped clean almost all of them [the stolen MS leaves of Bishop Otto] excepting where the writing would not come off et [*sic*] now I have much parchment to write down what I want is my own story even if I don't know to write Latin". He then wrote down in various languages, which he did not always understand, stories of his own invention; that they may allude to or gloss narratives told elsewhere, by Marco Polo in Italo Calvino's *Invisible Cities,* also allows us to see what has been called a

---

12 When an area of Piccadilly Gardens in Manchester, UK, was redesigned, for example, there was no way of seeing what had been there: see *Groundswell,* pp.48–51.

Preliminary orientations **9**

paratext at work (this is taken up in the next paragraph). Baudolino's auditor, Niketas the patient historian for whom he invents a host of lively and very convincing stories, questions him as to their veracity, and Baudolino replies, "Yes and No"; when Niketas says of Baudolino that "you are proud of your inventions", Baudolino responds, "But I made [my listeners] happy". Then after Baudolino's departure (having been punished for actually telling the unvarnished truth for once), the historian Niketas, pondering all of the other's miraculous and compelling stories, wonders how he – as a *bone fide* and professional historian – can put them into his own historical narrative, since he cannot credit such "lies". But he is reassured that "in a great history little truths can be altered so that the greater truth emerges".

The palimpsest has also been taken up by a literary theorist, Gérard Genette.[13] What he calls "paratextuality" concerns everything "that sets the text in a relationship, whether obvious or concealed, with other texts" (p.1); he lists five types of paratexts where another text is invoked or subjoined to the main one, and these all have their equivalent in modern landscape architecture – by quotations (including plagiarism) and allusion (copying or quotation – in our case of earlier design forms), by texts that are marginal to the central one (notes, epigraphs, forewords, even book covers, guide books, or garden pamphlets), by a specific taxonomic reference (invoking a particular genre, like a tragedy, or in our case, a park, a cemetery or some other cultural mode), by commentaries, and by the reference by one text (A) to another (B) that is more than commentary (as with Joyce's *Ulysses*). Genette quotes another critic, Michel Riffaterre, to the effect that "intertextuality is … the mechanism specific to literary reading" (p.2): but that is not necessarily the case, and many examples of gardens and landscapes perform in ways that reflect Genette's taxonomy, and that will be useful in what follows. By extension, Genette's paratexts might be augmented with the notion – relevant to gardens and parks that are located in specific places – of "displacement", where one place is referenced by another place elsewhere.[14]

We should think of both Eco's vision of palimpsest and Genette's literary paratextuality when we explore some "fabricated" or invented histories in landscape architecture. I am assuming in some of the gardens and landscapes that follow – Désert de Retz, Jardin Atlantique, Parc Bercy, Parc des Buttes Chaumont, and

13 Gérard Genette, *Palimpsests: Literature in the Second Degree,* trans. Channa Newman and Claude Doubinsky (Lincoln, NE: University of Nebraska Press, 1997). I am grateful to Sarah Katz for drawing my attention to the usefulness of this text for historical sites. Others have seized on this idea: Craig Owen in "The allegorical impulse: Towards a theory of postmodernism", *Beyond Recognition: Representation, Power, and Culture,* eds. Scott Bryson *et al.* (Berkeley, CA: University of California Press, 1992), argues that "One text is read through another, however fragmentary, intermittent or chaotic their relation may be" (p.53). And so with gardens, as will be seen.
14 I owe this suggestion to Matthew Dallos: displacement, as will be seen below, may apply to the Jardin Atlantique in Paris or to Teardrop Park in Manhattan, in both of which the site itself involved the displacement onto it of places elsewhere.

10 Preliminary orientations

others in Paris – that a particular site requires that we invoke something outside it or far away in time and space, or that the fabrication of a little truth may enable a greater site to emerge. In the many transformations that designers engineer, the actual and invented layers contrive landscapes that – give or take our different responses (*de gustibus non est disputandum*) – are believable and indeed "true". And this transformation of some invented place into true fact is, of course, a measure of all great art; it makes of invention, or what Shakespeare called "feigning" or pretending, the truest artistic creation. The fool Touchstone has it right, when in *As You Like It* he says that "the truest poetry is the most feigning". So perhaps, with gardens: truth may well lie in the palimpsest, both feigned and real.

The art of historical memory, by which we recover time, is a forgotten or at least difficult activity today, which is perhaps why we relish feigned histories.[15] We no longer know or rely upon the mediaeval and renaissance technique or system of the *ars memoria*. The traditions and habits by which classical rhetoricians and their successors explained and practised the arts of memory – situating their ideas in different parts of buildings or landscapes – seem useless in our very different culture: a culture with no educational insistence on training memory, and apparently far less need to do so systematically in an age when we have abundant paper and pencils (which the ancients did not possess), as well as palm pilots, portable recorders, PowerPoint projectors, video, Google, photography, tapes, etc. Nowadays we possess what I'd call an artless memory instead of an *ars memoria*. At best, we have a plenitude of memories, with no ready *method* of recalling and ordering them, or they are quickly searchable on a smartphone.

One analogy sometimes cited for our recovery of historical meanings is how psychoanalysis helps one to probe the past of individual memory. In Sigmund Freud's discussion of the mind's resources, he imaged it as some palimpsestial model of the ancient city of Rome: "in mental life nothing which has once been formed can perish – that everything is somehow preserved and that in suitable circumstances … it can once more be brought to light".[16] The metaphor may work at least for archaeologists and can be used when and if landscape architects need to ascertain what lies beneath their proposed new designs (some states in the USA require archaeological explorations to be undertaken before places are destroyed or remodelled). But otherwise it is less useful as a model for creating a palimpsestial landscape than as a tool for psychoanalysis.

It was this plenitude of possible meanings today that was cited by Bernard Tshumi when he made his presentation of the Parc de la Villette in Paris in the 1980s: he writes that "The world for us has become infinite, meaning that we cannot refuse it the possibility to lend itself to an infinity of interpretations". Tschumi himself then declared that his Parc de la Villette project "aims to unsettle

---

15 See Mary J. Carruthers, *Book of Memory: A Study of Mediaeval Culture* (Cambridge, UK: Cambridge University Press, 1992), and *Mediaeval Cult of Memory: An Anthology*, ed. Mary J. Carruthers (Philadelphia, PA: University of Pennsylvania, 2002).
16 *Civilization and its Discontents*, trans. James Strachey (New York: Norton, 1961), p.16.

both memory and context".[17] But, if we are then all set and happy to unsettle both historical memory and its contexts, landscape architecture is free to improvise, which Tschumi did at Parc de la Villette. Yet where this leads us is to a landscape practice where history is present but no longer coded and conveyed through some system like the *ars memoriam*. And thus a notion of an "invented" history does remain plausible and possible.

It was in fact Friedrich Nietzsche, whom Tschumi was certainly recalling or perhaps misreading, who isolated three different kinds of historian in his essay "On the uses and disadvantages of history for life".[18] For landscape architecture this triad could mean a monumental history – perhaps Halprin's FDR Memorial; the narrative of an antiquarian historian – any commentary on any historical garden that seeks to understand its original significance; and finally a critical history, that seeks to understand and respond to some event, which is what an 'invented' history may attempt. Indeed, the landscape architect has a particular role to play in a critical history: to be inventive, thoughtful and imaginative, able to pillage an endless memory bank of history for his or her work and not afraid to exploit it, able to find apt sites and, even more, apt figurations for them, and so to re-invent a new historical ground.

It can similarly be said that, as no person is without that deep layer of unconscious that Freud invokes (whether that person is aware of it or not), there can be no garden or landscape that is without history. Even something completed yesterday (none are, of course, ever "finished") has a history that began with the designer's understanding of the place where he wanted to build. In the pages that follow, I am concerned with something more substantial, a "deep history" rather than a person's unconscious memory bank. There will undoubtedly be very good examples of very recent work where that historical ground is not evident; indeed, many designs that I enjoy seem to have no obvious claim upon my historical interest or imagination: I mean no disrespect for those. But the thrust of this book *does* concern historical ground and a grounded history: for one essential reason, namely that it touches upon our need for locality.

Most people, even those who travel endlessly or move their base frequently, have some inclination for a place that is (even temporarily) home: one of the root meanings of nostalgia is that it is a memory of a lost or abandoned place or home. Now history is not nostalgia, though it can be motivated by it: rather historical ground is a place to which things adhere – memories of events, myths, physical items that people the landscape. It can be what the French poet and critic, Yves Bonnefoy, describes in his discussion of "place": "le lieu est le miroir où la vérité

---

17 *Cinegram Folie,* 1987, pp.I and VIII respectively.
18 To be found in *Untimely Meditations,* trans. R.J. Hollingdale (Cambridge, UK: Cambridge University Press, 1983); I owe this reference to Graham Larkin, "On the advantages of Nietzsche for garden history", *Studies in the History of Gardens and Designed Landscapes,* 20 (2000), pp.1–5. See also Peter Preuss, *On the Advantages and Disadvantages of History for Life* (Indianpolis, IN: Hackett Publishing, 1980).

12 Preliminary orientations

humaine peut apparaître..." ("Place is the mirror where human truth can appear...")[19]. He would further extend "lieu" to be a "haut lieu", the French word for a significant (not just a high) place, which is perhaps what I search for in historical ground.

All gardens and all landscape architecture are rooted (literally) in one particular place, one locality. A design that could be downloaded anywhere is unlikely to be a good design. Locality can be, so to speak, discovered or intuited on a site and then augmented by the designer – and, as we shall see, locality can mean different things in those instances. In rare cases, a design can wholly invent a new locality, and this may turn out to be, mysteriously, just what that place needed to make itself felt and recognizable.

One term for locality used to be "genius loci", genius of the place, a term that that been much derided today: the French philosopher Alain Roger thinks that "genius loci" does not exist and is simply what we ourselves attribute to a place but which has no physical existence of its own. (This is similar then to Richard Payne Knight who believed that nothing was "picturesque" in itself, but only something we discovered in it[20]. A rationalist may well accept that a place has no "genius", but it is itself somewhat nonsensical. We know about places because, not only do we recognize them and their topographical features, but we sense something about them that is special – we know about their past or things that have happened there, we recognize signs of something we think mattered at that place, and we find ways of ascribing those past events physically to it. Sure, we may be kidding ourselves and inventing a *genius loci* that is only our own projection. This may simply be a sentimentality, a nostalgic need to attribute something to a place that otherwise offers us nothing. But common sense and human experience allow that we can find in places something that has not been knowingly put there. And a designer can also do that, and invest a place with something special of his or her own devising that, because of what we ourselves see and experience there in the design, gives to that place its own *genius loci*.

There are in fact two kinds of *genius loci*. They are often confused or blurred, and Alexander Pope's famous articulation of *genius loci* ("consult the genius of the place in all....") in his *Epistle to Burlington* of 1731 seems to do precisely that.[21] There are the possibilities of a site: its waters, plants, topography, the place itself. And there is what we ourselves do to it, in practice or in our imagination, which changes it and

---

19 "Existe-t-il de 'Hauts' Lieux?", *Entretiens sur la poésie* (Paris: Mercure de France, 1990), pp.352–9.

20 I have discussed this in *The Picturesque Garden in Europe* (London: Thames & Hudson, 2002), pp.72 ff. On *genius loci* I use the unpublished essay by my late friend Michel Baridon, who argued it in his essay "Le Génie du Lieu et la naissance du jardin paysager". For Alain Roger, *Court traité du paysage* (Paris: Gallimard, 1997), pp.20 ff. See also Augustine Berque's discussion of what he terms "médiance", the art of milieu, which is not a place itself but how we envisage it: *Médiance: de milieu en paysages* (Montpellier, France: Reclus, 1990).

makes its new. Pope's lines expound the site itself, with falls of water, springs that "rise" in the landscape, hills, wood and glades; but there is also what the "genius" helps it to do – *directing* the waters, exaggerating a hillside with terraces, *opening* woodlands, catching echoes of answering glades, groves and shadows. Given that Pope was addressing Burlington, it seems possible that the "genius" is a maker like Burlington, or like Pope's friend William Kent, who was associated with Burlington; *the* Kent who eight years later would make waters "rise" in jets down the Vale of Venus at Rousham and "scoop" the Oxfordshire hillside there into a "theatre". The genius is equally a person who *envisages* how a landscape might look, as Pope does and which some of Kent's sketches do even before he got to implement his projects.

One key ingredient in the earlier understanding of "genius of place" was that it was called "histories". The term was used by the Royal Society in England, founded in 1662 and dedicated to a whole range of empirical enquiry.[22] Speci- fically, the Society promoted an interest in local history, recovering the meaning and association of places, mapping their terrain, listing and identifying monuments, ruins and other archaeological remains and records of antiquity. One of its members, Henry Oldenburg, drew up a document on which to base "inquiries for all Counties" in England – asking about such items as "air, water, earth, plants, animals, minerals, and famous inhabitants of particular locales".[23] And though it has been neglected in discussions of the picturesque, the new scientificism associated with the Royal Society contributed markedly to what came to be termed the picturesque, which provided a means of viewing and assessing landscapes, offering a complex language and syntax for looking, drawing and writing about the surrounding landscapes.[24] In short, a kind of history. We have forgotten that the picturesque was a means of understanding how the land looked, but was *not* a

21 In Pope's "Epistle to Lord Burlington", published in 1731. Lines of this are also quoted below in Chapter Two. For Rousham see the section on this garden in my *William Kent: Landscape Garden Architect: An Assessment and Catalogue of his Designs* (London: Zwemmer, 1987).

22 This is a topic not explored, as far as I know, in any discussion of the picturesque. For the Royal Society, see Charles Webster, *The Great Instauration: Science, Medicine & Reform 1626–1660* (London: Duckworth, 1975), Michael Hunter, *Science and Society in Restoration England* (Cambridge, UK: Cambridge University Press, 1981), and his essay on "John Evelyn in the 1650s" in *John Evelyn's "Elysium Britannicum" and European Gardening*, ed. Therese O'Malley and Joachim Wolschke-Bulmahn (Washington, DC: Dumbarton Oaks, 1998), pp.79–106. For work on two precursors of the Royal Society and their work in landscape, see *Culture and Cultivation in Early Modern England: Writing and the Land*, ed. Michael Leslie and Timothy Raylor (Leicester, UK: Leicester University Press, 1992) and *Samuel Hartlib and Universal Reformation: Studies in Intellectual Communication*, ed. M. Greengrass, M. Leslie, and T. Raylor (Cambridge, UK: Cambridge University Press, 1994). See also the CD-ROM edition of *The Hartlib Papers: A Complete Text and Image Database* (Ann Arbor, 1995).

23 Royal Society Classified Papers, XIX, no.43. Also published in Robert Boyle, *General Heads for the Natural History of a Country, Great or Small; Drawn out for the Use of Travellers and Navigators* (London, 1692).

14 Preliminary orientations

pictorial *model* for creating one. Paintings (and hence the picturesque) were essentially a tool for comprehension, for learning how to look, how to seize the substance of a place, to parse what you saw in the landscape, and learn about its components and to reflect upon them.

So locality concerns both the "histories" of physical forms and what we do for it by way of understanding, as well as by modifying it physically. This should seem self-evident. But it is rare that designers set out – though Pope appears to do it – this double understanding of locality or "genius loci". One of the most interesting contemporary landscape architects in Mexico, Mario Schjetnan, does exactly that. He premises his handbook on the principles of urban design (*Principios de Diseño Urbano/Ambienta*[25]) by surveying climate, time, geology, soils, hydrology, topography and vegetation – the physical genius of place – before he then proceeds to suggest ways of designing urban sites himself. These basic principles are what historical ground must take up as its fundamental condition.

24 See Emily T. Cooperman and John Dixon Hunt, "The American translation of the picturesque", forthcoming in a volume of essays on American borrowing from foreign lands, a form of palimpsest, *Foreign Trends in American Soil*, ed. Raffaella Fabiani Giannetto.
25 Written with co-authors Jorge Calvillo and Manuel Peniche (Mexico: Limusa, 1984).

2
HISTORY AS GEOLOGY, TOPOGRAPHY AND WEATHER

When Alphonse Alphand in the later 19th-century wrote his account of garden history to introduce *Les Promenades de Paris*, he was assuming that a designer might still be able to consider a site undisturbed by human intervention, as was suggested in the previous chapter. However, even if that were the case, he insisted that the designer still needed to study the site, since the place, its geology and its topography, had a historical hinterland. "Le relief du terrain est la première chose à étudier ... surtout quand le terrain est nu. Elle doit indiquer ... le mouvement des vallées, determiner le lit des rivières, l'emplacement des pieces d'eau, c'est-à-dire les parties capitals du plan" ("the lie of the land is the first thing to study ... above all when the terrain is bare; notably indicating the shape of valleys, determining the beds of river, water features, which is to say the central elements of the [proposed] plan"). He continued by listing the natural accidents of the site, which might determine the principal aspects of the new design; however, reworking the earth "pour composer un relief de fantasie est un mauvais système qui aboutit, presque toujours, à une deception, après d'énormes dépenses" ("to compose a plan out of one's fancy is a bad system that will almost always deceive and incur enormous expenses"; see ibid. p. xlix). He may well have been thinking of an earlier landscape architect, Jean-Marie Morel, also trained as an engineer, like himself, at the Ecole des Ponts et Chaussées. Morel, the first designer to be called a landscape architect ("*architecte-paysagiste*"),[1] was

---

1   See Joseph Disponzio, "Jean-Marie Morel and the invention of landscape architecture", in *Tradition and Innovation in French Garden Art*, ed. John Dixon Hunt and Michel Conan (Philadelphia, PA: University of Philadelphia Press, 2002), pp.137–59. Morel's book, *Théorie des jardins,* published in 1776, with a second edition in 1802, has never been translated, but the author's command of both natural sciences and their application to topography make him a pioneer in *ecological* assessment of landscape (though he never used the word).

16 History as geology, topography and weather

an expert at "identifying, interpreting, and recording" the components of landscape, and his analyses of landforms were based upon his engineer's instinct and his knowledge of the processes of the natural world. This attention by two masters of topography, with a substantial understanding of the deep history of a site, is what concerns this aspect of historical ground.

In three major respects, history impacts a site even before the designer makes his proposals for it: geology – the deep and long narrative of the earth's development; topography – the lie of the land as we see and explore it visually and on foot; and what shapes the surface of the land and its materials that we live with – the climate and the weather. For if we accept that weather is also a consequence of time – the French word "le temps" usefully means both weather and time – then history equally writes itself through weather and planting as well as through time. All three contribute to an essential history of place; yet all three are interconnected.

Nature's features and their changes over time tell us many things, and often these announce a narrative that contains or implies a history. A naturalist, Ken Weber, takes us on a ramble through Rhode Island:

> The route described here … is likely to keep you interested. You start near a tiny cemetery, pass another graveyard (surrounded by a picket fence) hidden far back in the woods, visit a couple of old cellar holes, take a look at a campsite for canoeists along the Pawcatuck River, pause in a clearing where apple and pear trees continue to survive long after abandonment, and walk along fields planted for the benefit of wildlife.[2]

This ramble is replete with an understanding of how we can see into the past ("the depth of time"). Yet this history emerges through how it is narrated, even if the instinct and intent of the writer is not itself historical. Other narratives will tell of changes in natural features, even plant physiology:

> As a leaf ages, the growth hormone, auxin, fades, and cells at the base of the petiole divide. Two or three rows of small cells, lying at right angles to the axis of the petiole, react with water, then come apart, leaving petioles hanging on by only a few threads of xylem. A light breeze, and the leaves are windblown.[3]

We respond to the dereliction of autumn, but in both the attention to how leaves behave botanically and in our awareness that this is a seasonal event, repeated every

---

2   Ken Weber, *Walks and Rambles in Rhode Island* (Woodstock, VT: Backcountry Public-ations, 1986), p.26. I owe this reference to Cheryl Foster, "The narrative and the ambient in environmental aesthetics", *The Journal of Aesthetics and Art Criticism*, 56/2 (1998), p.129, whose phrases I borrow here for my parenthesis and in-text quotation.
3   Diane Ackerman, *A Natural History of the Senses* (New York: Vintage Books, 1991), p.259. I also owe this citation to Cheryl Foster, ibid.

year, we are reading the "surface of the environment as a kind of story", and that narrative, too, involves us in an historical awareness.

Though he is not a landscape architect, Robert Macfarlane's exploration of walking[4] concludes his narratives of place with an unusual and inventive "Index of Selected Topics"; these include "Weather", different topographies ("Mountains and Hills", "Rivers and Streams") and geologies ("Rocks, Minerals & Earth"), along with other indices of things encountered and discussed. Few landscape architects are so specific or so focused about what constitutes a place; these topics constitute a true *genius loci*. Not every design acknowledges those phenomena, or, if they do, it may not readily communicate itself to its visitors, being rather a designer's preliminary enquiries than a visible statement of their presence once the site is established. But certainly for one landscape architect, Günther Vogt, these physical properties and encounters are fundamental to his published accounts of how he observes and explores landscape.

Geology

"Landscape as a phenomena [*sic*] is difficult to dismiss as mere phenomena, because the full story of natural *history* is too phenomenal, too spectacular, to be mere landscape". This paradoxical view that natural phenomena are not mere landscape ("it is a sacrament of something noumenal"[5]) is the truer if the perceiver is trained to observe. It is often geographers who can talk to us about these matters. The English geographer, Jay Appleton, wrote an intriguing piece on the role that geology played in the formation of picturesque landscapes in England.[6] He notes that it is "no exaggeration to say that comparatively little attention has been paid in the literature [of landscape architecture] to the nature of the underlying rocks, not least because the relevance of what is concealed from the eye is not always apparent" (p.270).

His detailed examination of the order and succession of rock-strata in a "Stratigraphical Column" is detailed and need not be repeated here. But his argument that sedimentary rocks are inclined to the horizontal, and resistant to weathering, and so tend to form escarpments, whereas less resistant marles and shales tend to form intervening vales, allows him to compare specific landscapes: the Great Avenue at Castle Howard, with the "Long Walk" in Windsor Great Park. Because the former (Figure 2.1) runs roughly north–south, the alternating summits and troughs of this switchback "successively expose and conceal the changing view ahead" (p.274), which is a typical experience of the picturesque. By contrast, the chalk land at Windsor provides an undifferentiated slope that, however pleasant,

---

4 *The Old Ways: A Journey on Foot* (London: Hamish Hamilton, 2012).
5 Holmes Rolston III, "Does aesthetic appreciation of landscapes need to be science-based", *The British Journal of Aesthetics,* 35 (1995), p.384, my italics.
6 Jay Appleton, "Some thoughts on the geology of the picturesque', *Journal of Garden History,* 6 (1986), pp.270–91.

18 History as geology, topography and weather

FIGURE 2.1 The Great Avenue, Castle Howard, Yorkshire, UK. The alternating summits and troughs are evidence of its geological formation.

somewhat lacks the same richness of movement by feet and eye. Once we have learnt from Appleton's careful adjudication of geological contributions in a landscape, it is relatively easier to appreciate, for example, how Chatsworth sits below an escarpment of Millstone Grit that effectively permits its water features (cascade and the Emperor Fountain) which a porous limestone would not do. The geology of other parklands may preclude extensive lakes, whereas outcrops of sandstone at Hawkstone, in Shropshire, have effected a site that its owners exploited for sublime thrills and picturesque play (hermits and ruins). Hence Appleton argues for the incidence of picturesque landscape effects that derive from geology in upland Britain rather than in the English lowlands. Geology makes palpable the topographical, the latent qualities that, formed in the distant past, become visible in the present and even the future.[7]

When Charles Eliot and Sylvester Baxter proposed their 1892 plan for a metropolitan park system in Boston it was premised on their understanding of the geology of the region.[8] Eliot saw the geological underlay of the city as a means of unifying its social and political territories, and he drew upon geology as a key

7   I am utilizing a remark by David Leatherbarrow in his discussion of topography, *Topographical Stories* (Philadelphia, PA: University of Pennsylvania Press, 2004), p.250. For a further insight into the "future" of the historical past, see my "Afterword/Afterlife".
8   I am indebted to Anita Berrizbeitia's talk on "Deep Time Made Visible: Charles Eliot and the Metropolitan Part System, Boston (1892–93)", unpublished paper read at the SAH Conference in April 2012, forthcoming in *Studies in the History of Gardens and Designed Landscapes* (2014). Quotations by Eliot are quoted from her text.

modern science: he recognized that "Upon the surfaces ... of well-rubbed rocks and the rounded heaps of glacial wreckage, fell rain and snow, which gathers itself into streams and sets out to sea ... [yet] wandering about in an usually aimless manner". This recognition of the geological history in Boston, Eliot also observes, makes it a "region of marvelously commingled waters, marshes, and gravel banks", which are then topographically reworked in massive transformations of the area – hills re-formulated, the Back Bay created by infilling marshes, and the tidal estuary of the Charles River transformed into a lake. It is an impressive diagnosis and, as Anita Berrizbeitia explains it, had a fundamental impact on how Eliot wanted to conceive Boston's cityscape. But his understanding of how deep time directed the "Diagram of parks and parkways" (a document from 1896) is not something that we perceive without the analyses of Eliot or, subsequently, of Berrizbeitia. As Martin J.S. Rudwick explains, the modern geological map is an attempt on "a two-dimensional surface [of] what cannot in reality be seen at all except in isolated exposures" on the land.[9] Specialists apart, we take geology largely on trust, even when it is carefully explained, because we cannot see it on or in the ground itself; we maybe see the meandering streams making for the sea around Boston, but even that incidental topography may not connect with the bigger, geological picture.

One modern design that is, however, particularly readable, because it simultaneously instructs and delights, is Paolo Bürgi's Geological Observatory at Cardada in the Canton of Ticino, Switzerland (Figure 2.2). Its name tells one immediately

FIGURE 2.2 Paolo Bürgi, The Geological Observatory, Cardada, Switzerland.

9   "A visual language for Geology", *History of Science,* 14 (1976), 149–95.

20 History as geology, topography and weather

that we are in a place where we should observe geology, and the vast arc of Swiss mountains seems to offer to visitors on its platform a considerable lesson, if we know how to look. Nonetheless, the ledge of the platform offers detailed images, plans and instructions on what lies before us. But it is the one, almost self-evident, item in the view itself that is most compelling, for the far mountain side is notable for a conspicuous cleft in the hillside. This slippage in the land marks the *insubric* line, which occurred millions of year ago when the European and African tectonic plates slipped past each other and ruptured the geology. Behind us on the circular platform, if we turn away from the view, are two lines of shapely stones: one consists of rocks from the African plate, the other those of the European.

Another compelling instance where an architect displays clearly a geological vision would be Luis Barragán's project for El Pedregal (The Rocky Place; Figure 2.3) in Mexico City (1945–50).[10] A suburban development was planned for some lava fields formed over 2,500 years earlier from nearby volcanoes. It was nonetheless a "bad land", home to snakes, scorpions and criminals; not a very propitious site, though inexpensive for development. But Barragán responded positively to the geology, the topography and the climate:"one advantage of these rocky formations is their fertility, the result of two important factors: first, the porosity and cracks produced in the rocks, with earth formed by dust laid over with millennia of rain; and second, the stable climate produced by the mild temperatures that preserved the rocks".[11] The dark soil, deposited by airborn particles, had promoted the growth of lichen, moss and flowers and grass. For some of the domestic enclosures Barragán removed the rough surface of hardened lava, on top of which, for his "demonstration gardens", he installed 40 centimetres of new topsoil.

Geology can allow designers unexpected opportunities that are immediately visible to the visitor because the designer has seized them and augmented them, and the geology itself informs the topography. The French landscape architect Bernard Lassus offers two examples. To create a new rest area at Nîmes-Caissargues, he was presented with a new *autoroute* that cut through the landscape on its way from Italy to Spain, the debris of which road-making was re-used to fill the quarry from which the materials had been taken.[12] On the flattened-out topography, which provided a considerable expanse of land, Lassus stretched a huge *tapis vert* (a green carpet, a

---

10 See David Leatherbarrow who discusses this site in *A Cultural History of Gardens*, vol.6, edited John Dixon Hunt (London: Bloomsbury, 2013), pp.187–9. He also noted that archaeologists had discovered very early settlements, which gave the site a strong historical resonance, an "emblem of Mexican identity".

11 *Barragán: The Complete Works,* ed. Raul Rispa (London: Thames & Hudson, 1996), p.35.

12 Each side of the *autoroute* has to be visited from different directions – you cannot explore both sides of the rest area at the same time. Lassus discusses this project in *The Landscape Approach of Bernard Lassus*, trans. S. Bann (Philadelphia, University of Pennsylvania Press, 1998), pp.164–7. There is an interesting discussion of this project, as a postmodernist perspective on the place as a "tourist" event, in Malcolm Woollen, "Nîmes-Caissargues Rest Area: a garden for non-dwellers", *Environment, Space & Place*, 1 (Fall 2009), 154–72.

History as geology, topography and weather 21

FIGURE 2.3 Luis Baragán, El Pedregal (The Rocky Place), Mexico City. (Copyright: Baragán Foundation, Switzerland. Artists Rights Society [ARS] New York, USA).

22 History as geology, topography and weather

typical French garden effect) on both sides of the roadway. That this "carpet" was higher than the roadway encourages a strange, palimpsestial experience of not knowing, historically, whether the highway or the expanse of grass was there first. But not content with the unexpected use of quarried materials, he also took advantage of the lie of the local topography, whereby a view of the city of Nîmes could be seen in the distance down the adjacent slope (Figure 2.4): to make visitors at the site understand what they saw in the distance he created two steel and grill belvederes on either side of the autoroute in the shape of the famous Tour Magne in Nîmes, each with maquettes of the Roman tower inside; along with the relocated façade of the Nîmes 19th-century opera house ("the first time that a classified historic monument had been moved to … a newly installed place"), the landscape allowed visitors to "conjure up the genuine presence" of the city below them.[13]

Elsewhere, at another rest area in the west of France at Crazannes, the engineers, pushing the road through the landscape, were confronted with the remains of limestone outcrops (Figure 2.5). Lassus was at first invited to sketch or invent some plausible cliffs that the engineers could create along the side of the road to provide a memorable feature for passing drivers. But as the roadwork continued, a world of excavated caverns was revealed that was even more impressive than any invented landscape; furthermore, research discovered that quarried material from this site had provided materials for innumerable famous buildings throughout Europe, from Cologne cathedral to the Arch of Germanicus at Saintes. Therefore stopping at an adjacent rest area, which is what Lassus then devised, allowed visitors to explore these caverns, and, as a rare fern (hart's tongue) was discovered in them, new walkways were constructed so that pedestrians would not disturb their habitat.[14] The revelation of these caverns, quarries which had provided stone for a variety of famous buildings elsewhere, as well as a rare plant on the floor of these caves, gave those who stopped their cars at this spot the chance to confront an otherwise missed historical event, that was both local and far away.

Invented topography, with glances at underlying geology, is perhaps more easily available today: Lassus eventually did not have to supply an invented scenography for Crazannes, because the "real" thing emerged. Yet for both of Lassus's rest areas it was the huge machinery of modern earth movers that enabled the smoothed out *tapis vert*, on the one hand, and the identification and presentation of the quarries, on the other. Where once wheelbarrows, buckets and large numbers of human labourers did the job of reforming a landscape like Cobham's Stowe in England during the early 18th century, huge machines can now totally and quickly refashion and emend what was originally there. Geoffrey Grigson captures both this and its historical irony when he wrote the four-line poem, "The Landscape

13 Lassus himself notes that "It is not my place to say whether the site will in fact work in this way" (p.167), but he recognized how the different factors – topography, "follies", the reference to Versailles's *tapis vert* – would construct an experience for the visitor.
14 Crazannes has been extensively documented by Michel Conan, *The Crazannes Quarries by Bernard Lassus* (Washington, DC: Dumbarton Oaks, 2004).

History as geology, topography and weather 23

FIGURE 2.4 A distant view of the city of Nîmes, France, from one of the Belvederes at the rest area, with a maquette of the Roman Tour Magne in the city, designed by Bernard Lassus.

FIGURE 2.5 The Quarries at the Crazannes rest area, France.

Gardeners", in which big yellow machines now "bite the given earth" as did rich Whigs in the 18th century who created lakes with massive human labour and said, truly, that "We are improving Nature".[15]

The "improvement" of nature can be easier with modern machinery, and also strangely unreal, although the Whiggish lakes must have seemed at the time a wondrous accomplishment (perhaps ironically, Alexander Pope praised the miracle of creating lakes – "The vast parterres a thousand hands shall make, / Lo! Bridgeman comes, and floats them with a lake"). Nowadays, the bulldozer has come into its own as a new "genius" of place.

Evidence of geology also makes its appearance in the work of Michael Van Valkenburgh. His Teardrop Park in lower Manhattan has a huge wall of layered bluestone, which (says a critic) is "reminiscent of the vertical cuts often seen on the thruways of upstate New York".[16] It is a dramatic and unexpected gesture (Figure 2.6) in a small space between apartment high rises, but its geological reference to upstate New York can necessarily only function as one of Genette's paratexts (via quotation, detail, allusion); or perhaps by displacement, since the wall, designed and tried out at full scale off-site, was then re-assembled in Manhattan,[17] far away from the "place" on upstate New York thruways.

15 *The Oxford Book of Garden Verse*, ed. John Dixon Hunt (Oxford, UK, Oxford University Press, 1993), p.248.
16 Erik de Jong, "Teardrop Park. Elective Affinities", *Reconstructing Urban Landscapes,* ed. Anita Berrizbeitia (New Haven, CT: Yale University Press, 2009), p.172.
17 See the illustrations of its construction in ibid, p.181.

FIGURE 2.6 Michael van Valkenburgh, Teardrop Park, New York. (Photo: Emily T. Cooperman).

Clearly, Van Valkenburgh loves the texture of stonework and how it maybe hints of geology; the bluestone paving on the Allegheny Riverfront Park in Pittsburg is indigenous.[18] More stacked bluestone at Bailey Plaza, Cornell University, is also homage to the region's Devonian-period sedimentary rock exposures. Modern machinery is able to position huge rockwork, evidences of geology not immediately present on site, like the slabs of unhewn marble at the Boston Children's Museum also by Van Valkenburgh, or the slabs of "quarried" stone (we see the marks of their blasting and excavation) for the sculptured element at Ourém Linear Park in Portugal, that – as evidence of geology – mediates between the geology, the urban tissue and the nearby brook.[19] These are subtle evocations of geological materials and the mining that produced them, and when situated in a landscape that has been expressively formed we tend to notice them. Whether Michael Heizer's "Levitated Mass", an immensely large boulder suspended over a long concrete trench outside the Los Angeles County Museum, can arouse in us a similar geological imagination seems far less clear.[20]

I resist invoking the innumerable ways in which building materials signal the history of a local geology, because I need to focus on landscapes themselves. But in

---

18 See *Michael Van Valkenburgh Associates: Allegheny Riverfront Park,* ed. Jane Amidon (New York: Princeton Architectural Press, 2005).
19 *PROAP. Arquitetura Paisagista* [Landscape Architectures] (Lisbon: NOTE Publishing), p.98.
20 See http://lacma.org/art/exhibition/levitated-mass (Heizer's work as a land artist is taken up briefly in Chapter Seven below).

26 History as geology, topography and weather

many ways the fragments of a landscape topography "persist as a remnant in finished works"[21] of architecture. David Leatherbarrow cites the examples of stones in the walls of Tavole House by Jacques Herzog and Pierre de Meuron that derived from a ruined building that once stood nearby, but before that "lay buried in nearby hills". His book provides a fresh commentary on the necessary dialogue between architecture and landscape, and it makes therefore many useful references to how the landscape is both enfolded into buildings as both historical material and with suggestions of landforms. A similarly strong sense of landscaped stones enfolded into a structure comes with the low line of the hotel designed by the architects Blacam & Meagar on Inis Meáin in the Aran Isles: its careful insertion of stones from the nearby beaches, gathered by the Irish owner himself, wrap around the low building, making a subtle and yet striking element in a famous and iconic landscape.

Geology invites several designers to explore and then proclaim a *longue durée* of historical time, whether or not it is endemic to the site. The Swiss landscape architect, Günther Vogt, is particularly fascinated by how his firm (and his students) explore both geology and topography.[22] Here, too, we encounter aspects of historical ground that "remain hidden from the superficial gaze" (*D&E*, p.12). His detailed exploration of the Yorkshire Dales or of the surroundings of the Hadspen House Estate in Somerset (*D&E*) link what are found on these walks, both the near – the photographs of fossilized corals and crinoids, the ravines and waterfalls – and the far (the distant fells, the geological and geomorphic aspects of land, its *karst*, or limestone pavements) to the designs proposed. At Hadspen, a long 7-day circular walk around the estate incorporated visits to a host of geological sites like Glastonbury, Cheddar Gorge, Wells and Stourhead; the exploration of this landscape is richly documented in maps and photographs, including graphs that show the visible horizon at every kilometre in order to document and narrate the process of walking through the landscape. What this exploration of a larger terrain showed was how poorly the estate itself was integrated into the national footpath network, and prompted Vogt to initiate this connection.

From the Somerset countryside to London's Parliament Square, the Vogt firm transposed the same awareness of a wide knowledge of English geology and topography onto this specific and historic place; besides celebrating the opportunities of a horizontal space, Vogt also "peeled away" the Westminster World Heritage Site to show 300 million years' worth of sedimentation, and a model of the Westminster geology sits on a plinth there: the model "helped us, and our clients, to think about the square as a geographical site rather than a listed monument" (*M&P*, p.73).

21 Leatherbarrow, pp.253 and 244 for the following reference.
22 There are two collections of his works, well illustrated and with excellent explanatory essays: Günther Vogt *et al.*, *Miniature and Panorama: Vogt Landscape Architects. Projects 2000–06* (Baden, Switzerland: Lars Müller Publishers, 2006) and Alice Foxley, *Distance and Engagement. Walking, Thinking and Making Architecture* (Baden, Switzerland: Lars Müller Publishers, 2010). References in the main text to these volumes are cited as *M&P*, *D&E*.

Physical exploration of ground is fundamental to Vogt, as it is, or should be, to other landscape architects; he appeals to the work of Hamish Fulton and documents his own dedication to walking and marking the rocks he discovered (*M&P*, pp.83–95).[23] Like Fulton's own images and documents, Vogt's publications insist upon the examination of both geology and topography, close-up focus and extended vistas, which can be registered in maps, graphs, photographs, and sketches. From these transects he brings to the Westminster project a newly realized awareness of England – that perhaps only a foreigner can have. It is a bravura exercise, rethinking landmarks, typical English footpaths and viewsheds, refiguring traditional Yorkshire pavements in modular format at Westminster, making surface channels inspired by drainage in the Lake District, and using copses from Somerset for a thoroughfare alongside St Margaret's Church. The 26-page sequence (*D&E*) that documents this wide-ranging and yet focused concern for the Westminster site explains more, I expect, than any visitor will be able to determine on site. The imaginative energy that underlies or sustains this project may only reveal itself slowly, like the ingredients of geology's deep and sustained evolution; meanwhile, there is some striking topography, rich, immediate and visually compelling that prompts and sustains that larger enquiry.

The formation of the earth, and its crust, are an ineluctable part of the history of a place, though we are often less attentive to this geology, unless it suddenly ups and strikes us in the face, like the White Cliffs of Dover, the mountains that rise above Lac Léman when seen across the lake from Vevey in Switzerland, the stratifications as we descend into the Grand Canyon, or the Pallisades in the South Plains of South Dakota. Geology being formed gradually over millions of years can escape us; deep time does not impact us dramatically. Sudden catastrophes, however, when earthquakes and volcanic eruptions occur and reformulate their locality, are shocking revelations of what hitherto we had probably neglected. Just occasionally, these effects can be simulated: at Bad Oeynhausen, famed for its healing waters or baths, Agence Ter/Henry Bava created a large fountain that bursts from the earth, within a Corten steel (gabion-lined) ring, as the Water Crater, a magical and visible aquifer.[24]

Topography

Topography is the more visible and tangible evidence of the earth's deep and long-sustained formation and of humanity's work upon it. The morphology of a terrain will be – or should be, as both Morel and Alphand insisted – the determinant of all design proposals. Topography is a framework for designed sites: "it continually makes ... traces of past performances that have sedimented themselves" into either landscape or buildings.[25] Sometimes, the surface of the land has been worked over

---

23 This is one instance of the impact of land art, among whom Fulton is to be counted, that I take up in my final chapter.

24 Agence Ter, *Territories* (Basel, Switzerland: Birkhäuser Architecture, 2008), pp.18–21,

25 David Leatherbarrow, *Topographical Stories*, p.12.

28 History as geology, topography and weather

by human beings, levelling fields, raising bulwarks and ditches, and making shorter-term manipulation more visible. This permanent manipulation of landforms is in distinct contrast to what happens to water, which is disturbed only briefly: whereas a boat glides over water that then resumes its shape and "erases all trace of passage", the "earth is more faithful and stores the marks of pathways that man had trodden. … The road stamps its mark on the soil and seeds shoots of life [sic]: houses and household, villages and cities".[26] This attention to what the earth tells us is similar to what Alexander Pope explains in his lines about the "genius loci" – that it is both (and ambiguously) the lie of the land itself AND whatever "genius" (designer, landowner) has directed its forms:

> Consult the *Genius* of the *Place* in all,
> That tells the Waters or to rise, or fall,
> Or helps th'ambitious Hill the Heav'ns to scale
> Or scoops in circling Theatres the Vale …

Topography is much more easily recognized outside urban areas – catching opening glades, joining willing woods. In cities we are maybe less affected by the topography: cities like Siena, though, impose their "irrationalities of design"[27] upon us by virtue of the conspicuous topography. Otherwise it is largely when we are climbing a steep hill, or peddling up an incline that we sense the topography. Montmartre in Paris and Telegraph Hill in San Francisco are exceptions, partly because they are visible before we encounter them. We can maybe guess that a distant view of New York with skyscrapers at mid-town and at the tip of Man-hattan, but not in between, hints at different geologies that do not easily sustain high buildings throughout the whole city. The seven hills of Rome are certainly noticeable when one arrives on the Palatine or climbs the Aventine, but there is so much to notice throughout the city that its topography is today less immediately conspicuous. However those hills were formed by the erosion of volcanic deposits flowing west into the Tiber River, and though those crests were settled first, human inhabitation over three thousand years has filled the floodplain and the interstitial valleys with modern buildings, urban debris and collapsed buildings that have changed the topography considerably.

Yet even in hills and mountains we can still miss the thrill or, perhaps more crucially, fail to grasp how our understanding of topography enables a richer sense of the past in a given landscape. Too many visitors just gaze from a safe mountain promontory, snap views with their cameras and then sit in a comfortable café with

---

26 Quoted PROAP, p.42; further quotations and references in this chapter are to this volume. As Leatherbarrow says, topography gives "amplitude and configuration to the settings and surroundings of practical life", both found and worked on (*Topographical Stories*, p.4).

27 The phrase is from Robert Hewison, *Eccentric Spaces* (London: Andre Deutsch, 1977), p.66.

familiar views; they "consume" the landscape, without feeling or understanding it. At Cardada, Paolo Bürgi wanted not only to alert visitors to momentous and distant geological events at his Observatory, but also to make them understand and feel the impact of the more immediate topography. So lower down the mountain, instead of clearing the trees on the mountainside to enable a panorama from a safe promenade, he created a dizzy platform that juts out over the treetops into the void – for me, at least, a fairly scary event that certainly requires me to respond to the view in a less routine way. But on the surface of the walkway, which somebody like myself much appreciated because I could look down and not always have to gaze out into the void, are etched symbols of ecology and the structures of living organisms: a maple leaf and a buzzard's footprint, the DNA symbol of a cell, the Fibonacci sequence (each new number equalling the sum of the previous two, "connected in an ecosystem"[28]). Bürgi himself wants this to be intriguing, to add "a sense of mystery", rather than to give visitors a lesson.

But his pedagogic skills are not to be gainsaid. He himself writes that "the *story* the project tells" (my italics) is not confined to either the platform or the Observatory, because "I believe that knowing something about the history of a landscape … can change your perception of it and transform it into a very different place". Hence his inscription of a poem by Jorge Luis Borges, "Nostalgia for the Present",[29] to be read on the handrail of the promontory; while on the path that leads from the platform towards the chair lift to the Observatory he installed what he calls a "Ludic Path". Here is a series of games that people can play to discover how the laws of physics work: a merry-go-round to explore centrifugal force, parabolic mirrors to communicate at a distance, a seesaw that utters sounds as you balance on it. And unusual benches along the path invite you to sit and grasp how the path climbs through four zones, each with a dominant tree type (silver fir trees, beech trees, larches, Norway spruce). Now all these elements on the Cardada mountainside are the evident signs that a landscape architect is also a historian of the place, narrating not only distant, historical events, but also ones that confront us directly as we walk through the landscape. And like Halprin, he is content to stimulate us with names ("geological observatory", "ludic path") along with words on the railings of the Observatory and to trigger our imagination with images that require identification. Yet the ultimate narrator is the visitor who responds to it and thus registers its history.

28 Bürgi's detailed programme and explanation for the Cardarda project, and others, are set out in interviews in *Paolo Bürgi Landscape Architect: Discovering the (Swiss) Horizon: Mountain, Lake and Forest,* ed. Raffaella Fabiani Giannetto (New York: Princeton Architectural Press, 2009). It is also Bürgi's phrase that people "consume" the Swiss landscape and do not really understand it. See also *Fieldwork,* pp.178–81.

29 It is probably the title of Borges's poem itself, not the contents, that seem to matter here; it begins "At that very instant…" but then addresses an absent girlfriend "inside the great unmoving daytime". So for the present it is our "nostalgia" of some past that is referenced here. The poem is from the volume, *The Limit,* in *Collected Poems,* ed. A. Colman (New York: Viking, 1999).

30 History as geology, topography and weather

Vogt's *Miniature and Panorama*, too, instructs us on how to appreciate both the far and the near. Like many a contemporary landscape architecture student, he presents us with a rich anthology of images, where dozens of miniature, close-up photographs reveal, variously, how people occupy spaces in parks, how 193 species can form a herbaceous border of 5,000 square metres, how dendrological trees-rings are revealed under a microscope; images of Swiss cloud formations, plants for heathlands, birch trunks, mosses, paving stones, narratives of succession on unused terrain in Basel, and endless close-ups that plunge our face into tree roots, topiary, bricks and clays. From these miniatures evolve panoramic designs for a variety of topographical formats in the different conditions of gardens, courtyards, parks, and cemeteries. Sports arenas in Munich, housing developments in Beijing, corporate HQs, interiors and warehouses are revealed as an ineluctable part of a much larger vocabulary of topographical forms that reveal the historical materials of their sites and local planting. This is a topography of carefully studied minutiae that sustains and illuminates a plenitude of new designs, where the historical "event" and the new "occasion" are indelibly entwined.

A Portuguese firm like PROAP also works hard to make the topography visible and related to its historical site ("topographical manipulation" represents an "essential parameter in the transformation of landscape"[30]), and a park is always a *re*design of something already existing. Since, for this firm, a landscape is a "portrait stamped upon the territory", then all "human convictions" become part of the landscape, whether urban or rural, ancient or recent: "roads, power lines, railways, dams and ports", but also agricultural fields, castles, villages and forests (*AP*, p.26). As noted in the first chapter, it seems easier to register these "human convictions" in European countries than in the United States: it was, after all, John Ruskin who thought (wrongly) that the instinct to appeal to ruins "can hardly be felt in America".[31]

At PROAP's City Park in Lagos, Portugal (Figure 2.7), a historic wall is drawn into a new parkscape between the old city and the massive growth of the new one, and this working space is formulated as an "emptiness, a place without functions or permanent physical content" (*AP*, p.107). This stage or "scenario" allows people to do what they want within the imposing site – yet another way in which a humble and subtle modern intervention draws the past into the usefulness of a future. Similarly, the hillside at Silves, also in Portugal, privileges necessarily the castle on its mound: acknowledging the archaeological vulnerability immediately below the walls, while also inserting two basic pragmatic elements – a new service building and a new entry through the castle walls, approached by pedestrian routes that

---

30 PROAP, *Arquitetura Paisagista* [Landscape Architecture] (Lisbon: NOTE, 2010), pp.11 and 25, with further references in the text (cited as *AP*).
31 *The Library Edition of the Works of John Ruskin,* ed. E.T. Cook and Alexander Wedderburn, 39 vols. (London 1903–12), V.369. Others who thought the same are noted in David Lowenthal, "The Place of the Past in the American Landscape", *Geographies of the Mind*, ed. David Lowenthal and Martyn J. Bowden (Oxford, UK: Oxford University Press, 1975).

FIGURE 2.7 PROAP, Lagos City Park, Portugal, 2003–2009: relation between the Castle and the park. (Courtesy of the designers).

bring people from the surrounding streets – which allow fresh views of the castle, and then, on their return, views of the city and countryside (*AP*, p.113).

Careful transitions between historical event and contemporary living, liminal segments, are inevitable in a landscape with a strong historical presence side by side with modern life and needs. Most clearly, these liminal insertions are conveyed by emphasizing different levels, or using different materials for the pathways – gravel or wooden decking. In the redevelopment of the Fenestrelle Fort in Turin – a large and prominent landmark with a complex of forts and other defensive structures from 1727 to 1850 – PROAP wanted to bring a "new human presence" onto the mountain and yet also use some recovered traditions of agriculture around the fortifications. The "course of history" (*AP*, p.35) is therefore, often writ large on a site, with ancient buildings or infrastructure, like the salt mines in Maras or Inca cultivation to which these designers point; yet the inscription of contemporary usages has also to be inserted and recognized in their designs. Nor is historical ground simply one topographical event, but a record of "successive generations" "repeated daily over long periods" (*AP*, p.43), another paratext or threshold that joins past to present and future. Their masterplan for the Promenade de l'Indépendance in Algiers also envisages a necessary use of historical ground for "the construction of the world in the XXI century" (*AP*, p.225): transversal streets from the historical centre that lead to the "deactivated" port envisage an intervention at once touristic and entertaining, yet symbolic (Figure 2.8). The topography of the urban terrain here proves to be determinant. Eager to

32 History as geology, topography and weather

FIGURE 2.8 PROAP, Masterplan for the Promenade de l'Indépendance, Algiers, 2007: access to the Monument. (Courtesy of the designers).

understand the "characteristics of the place" and unwilling to run "counter to the natural forces" that need to underlie their intervention (*AP*, p.9), PROAP's modelling of (especially) urban forms has consequences for shaping ecology, scenic values and public use that "establish the meaning of the prospective landscape: three-dimensional, diversified, rhythmic" (*AP*, p.61).

The PROAP firm argues that it was "artists engaged in landscape painting that showed bourgeois society that which it wanted to see" (*AP*, p.39). In this, they reprise the picturesque injunctions of Richard Payne Knight who approved of Humphry Repton's reliance on painters to train the eye to appreciate the lie of the land.[32] Today, if are lucky to find ourselves in an un-designed landscape, it is relatively easy to notice the shape of its valleys, water features (rivers, stream and waterfalls), cliffs, or rolling down land, whereas urban settlements, especially when viewed in close-up, can obscure the topography. But we can improve these visual skills, not only by observation, but by looking – as Repton realized – at the ways in which British water-colourists saw and depicted the landscape and its buildings. Their eye for topography is one of the most remarkable aspects of painters of landscape in the late 18th and 19th century: some, like Francis Towne dramatize the geological shapes, while others like John Sell Cotman observe how the land lies, how the streams flow, and the trees are formed within the landscape.[33] If a landscape is, further, studded (as it can be in Europe) with ancient edifices, castles,

---

32 This is cited by Appleton, above note 5.
33 I have found the wonderful anthology of images in *The Great Age of British Watercolours 1750–1880* (London: Royal Academy, 1993) a great stimulus when I am exploring similar landscapes.

History as geology, topography and weather **33**

ancient lanes and by-ways, derelict factories, dams that once had a function in providing water power, all of which were noticed by British water colourists, then we have an added incentive to recognize the historicity of that landscape's topography. Today, as with Vogt's imagery, photography has taken over from water colours, but without loss of detail of form, texture, colour, thickness, luminosity and topographical relationships.

A good example of how photography can alert us to topographical incidents that we might otherwise neglect is the photographic imagery of agricultural land in the German Ruhr, where new inhabitants have themselves learned how the topography is palpable.[34] As explained by Paolo Bürgi in *Feldstudien/Field Studies,* the designer needed to respond to a dual need – for farmers to sustain the livelihood of their land and for people in encroaching housing estates to find the adjacent farmland interesting. So he suggested that the land be ploughed with visible patterns of ploughing, grubbing and seeding; the transformed land has panels of poppies in the corn fields, cornflowers in the wheat fields, and in the winter months the marks of cultivation crossing the rolling landforms (Figure 2.9). The photographic images of these field studies suggest how wonderfully clear the otherwise ordinary looking agriculture appears now to the farmer's neighbours. Now the topography speaks to them too. For topography does need to declare itself more fully, to speak to its visitors; it may too often be just a remnant in finished work, lying "very absconded and deep" in a site.[35] When Elizabeth Meyer, in discussing how Vaux and Olmsted changed the boundaries of Prospect Park to include three glacial formations that then could be reinforced as distinct landforms – the meadow, the ravine and the lake – she argued that without knowledge of both geology and new landforms, the "ground is silent". In a witty turn of picturesque phrasing, she writes that "A site emerges from the *frame* of a landscape".[36]

Others designers have learnt to play with topography and make it immediate as well as new. Georges Hargreaves is particularly keen to parade these modulations in surface and texture, what Elisa Leviseur identifies as "Hargreaves weaves" (Figure 2.10).[37] His unmistakable syntax of mounds, berms, circular and spiral forms, and meandering paths is something that he says he needs in order to make people "read" the landscape, by which he intends both the site's physical history (invented or enhanced) and its narratives. In bulk, his work tends (for me) to be somewhat

34 *Feldstudien/Field Studies. The new aesthetics of urban agriculture* (Basel, Switzerland: Birkhaüser, 2010), pp.96–101. The whole of these studies, of which Bürgi's is but one, make clear the role of change, time, history that have been exploited in the new Ruhr farmlands.

35 Leatherbarrow, op cit., p.250, quoting the Third Earl of Shaftesbury.

36 Elizabeth Meyer, "The Expanded Field of Landscape Architecture", in *Ecological Design and Planning*, eds. George Thompson and Frederick Steiner (New York: Wiley, 1997), pp.45–97; my italics.

37 *The Architectural Review* (September, 1993), pp.80–4; quotations from Hargreaves, unless otherwise noted. Her title can mean either that he waves forms or that his weaving is what we notice, or both of course.

34 History as geology, topography and weather

FIGURE 2.9 Paolo Bürgi, re-envisaging the fields with new ploughing and sowing in the German Ruhr. (Courtesy of the designer).

History as geology, topography and weather **35**

FIGURE 2.10 George Hargreaves, Guadalupe River Park, San Jose, CA. (Courtesy of Hargreaves Associates).

monotonous: photographs of his work in the firm's substantial archive, *Landscape Alchemy*,[38] to which imagery he himself points (p.6) as the primary representation of his work, are magnificent, but have a cloying sameness; on the other hand, visits to individual sites, though immediately recognizable for their authorship (what Mario Praz called "the ductus" or hand writing of an artist[39]), manage to individualize the specific local history, site, ecology and public use.[40] Some of his responses to specific flood conditions are discussed below, more appropriately, under weather.

Weather

Weather is more difficult for designers to manipulate; they have to take whatever comes, whether storm run-off or "millennia of rain" (to quote Barragán again). The earth's crust is impacted by weather, or by climate which has also a long and

38 *Landscape Alchemy: The work of George Hargreaves*, with contributions by George Hargreaves, Julia Czerniak, Anita Berrizbeitia, and Liz Campbell Kelly (Novato, CL: ORO Editions, 2009). I resume discussion of Hargreaves in Chapter Five below.
39 Mario Praz, *Mnemosyne: The Parallel Between Literature and the Visual Arts* (Princeton, NJ: Princeton University Press, 1970), p.31.
40 This does suggest that firms who publish their own work – Hargreaves, Olin, Van Valkenburgh, Vogt, PROAP – are better served when they focus upon specific projects; this especially helps to make the history of a specific site clearer, especially when that topic – though mooted – is not much analysed amid displaying the firm's more generic and boosterish profile. Still, site visits do an even better job.

36 History as geology, topography and weather

changing history, and its influence on the earth's surface is considerable; but again we tend only to see this after heavy rainstorms, floods, extraordinary heat, or when snow covers the ground and suddenly surprises us with a sense of its topography. Weather conditions are all elements of an historical ground, and they impinge on our understanding of it. "We make mention of the wind, the sun and the shade" that depend upon our "actual sensation of comfort".[41] But the various manifestations of water – flooding, storms, rising level along waterfronts and seashores – could be cherished as more than casual elements of historical ground and can be, to some extent, manipulated. Climate change and rising water levels around coasts are one long-term weather condition that must be confronted by designers. And this further allows designers to address areas alongside water that, now derelict, can be enhanced and at the same time given protection from potential flooding.[42]

Safeguarding coastlines and river banks against tidal surges or flooding signals how weather and climate are matters that not only impinge on, but shape, the landscape. The Netherlands have long since adapted to the land's relationship with the sea, by using dykes to prevent flooding, but also by encouraging the fashion in which water, wetlands, swamps, reed beds, polders and coastal remains are treated and made visible; it provides one of the most noticeable examples of landscape architecture's focus upon topography and weather. In his essay on "Flatness", prefacing his firm's volume, *Mosaics*, Adriaan Geuze of WEST 8 offers an elegant review of Dutch battles with sea and drained lands ("landscape fashioned from the bottom of the sea"). Few landscape architects could manage as rare and poetic narrative as this history of this "Nieuwe Land" (new land), at once attentive to the religious culture of its Calvinism ("the soul of the people who had succeeded in creating the polder land had yearned for a religion that would provide salvation from the difficult existence below the waves"), and to its engineers, painters, landscapists and photographers who created and celebrated this astonishing landscape, whose showpiece polder at Noordoost aptly earned designation by UNESCO as a World Heritage Site. Geuze also delivers a stunning and at times forensic denunciation of the modern erasure of this historical land by the joint and brute forces of lawyers, system manager and municipalities who worked to erase "the collective memory of the culture". Not surprisingly, WEST 8 has paid careful attention to this dimension of Dutch landscaping: his early and famous Nature Reserve at Oosterschelde used strips of black and white mussel shells along the weir, perhaps an allusion to the oblong parcels between drainage ditches on polder

---

41 PROAP, *AP*, p.19.
42 Written in the immediate aftermath of Hurricane Sandy in November 2012, this sounds naïve: we need to safeguard low-lying areas, because only then can people live in safety, rather than "sit it out" with dangerous consequences, while still enjoying extremes of weather.

land, as well as a homage to the geometries of Mondrian.[43] His more recent project for the Leidsche Rijn Park,[44] to the west of Utrecht, re-excavates a meander of the River Rhine and, within a 5-kilometre wall, establishes a "Binnenhof" (courtyard) of waterways. This "secretive inner world" is designed for a new residential district of 35,000 homes that emphasizes this land of water, as well as woodland and walkways, and secures it within a typical Dutch courtyard typology.

With the onslaught of climate change, designers are confronting the necessity to respond to it. Yet in the Australian publication, *Climate Design*, where planning is addressed, it seems far easier to isolate how and why climates have changed than to contemplate design for these new conditions.[45] Their approaches focus on food and agricultural systems, with eloquent appeals to philosophy, theology and chaos theory, but are short on design solutions. The hope for "a great philosophical work of landscape architecture" in the 21st century appears to depend upon "reconciling the sky with the ground" (i.e. reconciling the chemical composition of the atmosphere, rather than God, with us, earthly humans). It is in such "reconciliations" that we will presumably discover physical forms and moments of apprehension, and maybe even "great" new works on the ground.

While some people find issues of climate puzzling not to say unproblematic, weather is noticed by everybody. Van Valkenburg's wall at Teardrop Park oozes water that freezes in winter and changes the whole of the rockface. Similar devices – screens of wire on which the descending water freezes – were also used by Van Valkenburg in Boston, and Ken Smith had a similar ice screen of wires in Yorkville Park, Toronto. Such palpable hints of season in northern climates are even more telling than autumn foliage and flowers, in part because in cold climates these evidences of winter can last longer and are not covered with snow; they are also somewhat unexpected on the forms that have been contrived for them.

An even more modest proposal for acknowledging weather, specifically rainfall, was made by Günther Vogt for a hotel in Zürich. The "Weather Garden" (Figure 2.11) at the Park Hyatt Hotel calls attention to the times and variations of the weather. An interior courtyard, which visitors cannot enter but only look down on

---

43 The Oosterschelde site is also illustrated as figure 86 and a comparable polder landscape in figure 51 in my *Greater Perfections: The Practice of Garden Theory* (Philadelphia, PA: University of Pennsylvania Press, 2000). The Dutch attention to the special conditions of their landscape is addressed in *Het Landschap* [The Landscape] Katrien van der Marliere, ed. (Antwerp: deSingel, 1995, especially pp.215–51 and in Ter Agence, *Territories*, pp.84–5 and 102–5.

44 Images, plans, models and early planting can be seen in WEST 8, *Mosaics* (Basel, Switzerland: Birkhäuser Architecture, 2008), pp.28–47. See also *Fieldwork: Landscape Architecture Europe*, ed. Landscape Architecture Europe Foundation (Basel, Switzerland: Birkhäuser Architecture, 2009), pp.144–53, and Tim Richardson, *Avant Gardeners: The Visionaries of the Contemporary Landscape* (London: Thames & Hudson, 2008), p.129, for other work that acknowledges interventions in Dutch polder landscapes.

45 See *Climate Design: Design and Planning for the Age of Climate Change*, with the collaboration of Peter Droege (Australia: ORO Editions, 2009). The subsequent quotation is by Richard Weller, p.31.

38 History as geology, topography and weather

FIGURE 2.11 Günther Vogt, The Weather Garden, Park Hyatt Hotel, Zürich. (Copyright: Christian Vogt).

from their hotel rooms, is paved with a dimpled stone grid where the reflected rainclouds, the downpours, the transforming puddles and the evaporating water make the story of rain tangible and evocative.[46]

Like freezing curtains of ice, we also accept, and indeed even have a chance of celebrating, floodwaters. In the past, landscape architects shied away from river fronts – because of industrial shipping, though that has largely disappeared, and now because of the unsightliness of these derelict areas, and because of the danger of flooding. But more and more fluvial parklands are being established, sometimes braced against potential flooding by walls and bulwarks that protect an inner parkland. With steadily warming climates and rising sea levels, such measures seem wise. And one telling mark of this fresh attention to the excitements of water are the uses of floating pathways, as at the Parque do Tejo e do Trancão in Lisbon,[47] or the walkways laid across the flooded quarry at the Shanghai Botanical Garden, that rise and sink with the level of the waters.

Mill Race Park, in Columbus, IN (Figure 2.12), an early project by Van Valkenburg, had customarily been forced to tolerate frequent flooding of the Flatrock and Driftwood Rivers that merge to form the White River. But with the new design the cycles of the floods could be incorporated into the life of the park – not something simply to be tolerated, but fundamental to its new life and shape and its necessary dialogue with park users. Two gravel pits were converted into ponds, the higher one of which, a perfect circle, is the last to be inundated and the first to emerge from the sinking river waters. In the dry season, an amphitheatre and adjacent forms in the landscape, like the circular pond, are the modest insertions into this parkland that accepts its new liminal existence between dry land and water. It makes – perhaps another Genette paratext – a modern version of that historical moment of the third day in *Genesis,* when the dry land was divided from the waters and the earth brought forth grass, and when, later in *Genesis*, the flood temporally overwhelmed the earth.[48]

At Guadalupe River Park, in San José, CA, another early project by George Hargreaves also confronts the three-mile river by assessing the volume and speed of the water flow that can flood the city.[49] Rather than accept the recommendation by the Army Corps of Engineers to control flooding with 17-foot concrete floodwalls, Hargreaves, with their collaboration, organized a process by which wildlife could be saved in the city, storm water allowed to infiltrate the site, and a

---

46 I am grateful to Tyler Swanson for drawing this site to my attention, since when I have become absorbed with Vogt's designs.

47 See PROAP, *AP*, pp.61 ff. for the discussion and detailed images and sketches.

48 There is a striking similarity between the rising and the receding waters of Mill Pace Park and the nearby Miller gardens that Dan Kiley designed, where a stream floods the lowest part of the lawn, a liminal threshold where wet and dry land constantly inter-change. Given that apparently Kiley once suggested linden trees on the site of Mill Race in the 1960s (*Reconstructing Urban Landscapes*, p.47), the parallel may not be accidental.

49 I am indebted here to *Landscape Alchemy,* pp.16 ff.

40 History as geology, topography and weather

FIGURE 2.12 Michael Van Valkenburgh, Mill Race Park, Columbus, IN. (Courtesy of Landslides Aerial Photography).

riparian planting system was created that provided a recreation corridor. The design allows the river to "perform", even to display itself through a manipulation of the depth and width of its flows; a variety of gabions, steps and terracing, along with one concrete wall, are visible indications of how the river is encouraged to reveal itself at different times and in different forms as its passes through the city. Landforms and pathways can be inundated, while the shapes of the surrounding land mimic the topographical conditions through which the river flows. With its emphatic display of undulating banks and wave-like berms that protect the city, while ensuring that people have a viable corridor for recreation, the project presents a "catalogue of design solutions for specific circumstances employed wherever necessary" (*Landscape Alchemy*, p.6). Indeed, both here and somewhat later at the Louisville Riverfront Park, KY, where Hargreaves transformed a postindustrial land, he delights in strong gestures and bravura forms; these exaggerate the topographical forms, and thereby our attention to them, while responding to the specific demands of a dialogue between land and water. A sloping lawn now acts, unlike the original 20-foot flood wall, as a site for temporary inundation: the landscape forms and uses a historical narrative of how natural processes and human responses converge.

PROAP, too, has been much concerned with both fluvial parklands and riverfronts, in both of which an acknowledgement of weather and its changes is paramount. For the Quinta do Alamal Fluvial Park in Gavião, with a river flooded as a result of a new dam, and now pacified by other small weirs and lagoons, the river is both contained, with a new beach area, and able to tolerate rising levels of water. Here too there are floating walkways (*AP*, pp.69-73). The Barcelos Fluvial Park (Figure 2.13) also engineered new connections between river and city, and between different levels alongside the river itself and the land behind reached by platforms and stairs.[50]

On a much more pragmatic scale, storm-water treatments have begun to be increasingly rendered so that the visitors can appreciate the very visible effects and result of downpour; this in turn alerts people to the incidence of weather patterns rather than having masses of surplus water disappear unnoticed and often toxic into the ground; whether these infrastructures also suggest more understanding of weather patterns is open to question, but the materials for comprehending these historical moments have been made much more visible and in many cases more attractive. For a housing estate in Lakewood Hills, Windsor, CA, Hargreaves uses two-foot-high weirs to catch the storm water in rushing cascades after heavy rainfall.[51]

FIGURE 2.13 PROAP, Barcelos Fluvial Park, Portugal, 2004–2009: topographical elements. (Courtesy of the designers).

50 *AP*, pp.133–5. See also their project for the south bank of the River Mondego in Coimbra, Portugal (pp.141–3), where there is another floating pathway across the water.
51 See *Architectural Review*, 12 (1993), pp.81 and 83.

42 History as geology, topography and weather

A web site (http://www.artfulrainwaterdesign.net) offers an intriguing variety of further examples that urge greater satisfaction for their "amenities", yet also demonstrate an elegant presentation of how storm water, roof run-off, or hydrology generally can be presented to the public. Cedar Run Education Center in Washington State conducts its run-off down a picturesque meander where the water is clarified and enhanced under a perforated steel cover; a storm-water system for Frank Gehry's MIT Stata Center regulates flow and recycles it through a wetland that the Olin Studio claimed as invoking "a slice of new England" for its riverine system (Figure 2.14); the Tanner Springs Park in Portland, OR, allowed people and wildlife into the new Pearl District neighbourhood; this involved much interaction with local communities, a process that sharpened local appreciation of the new ecology.[52]

Time is cognate with weather, for both impact the earth's core and its surfaces. But time and weather reveal themselves in other ways. To start with, the garden is never fixed or "static", as Michel Beaujour claims[53] – except, maybe, in very rare

FIGURE 2.14 Olin Studio, stormwater management, M.I.T. Stata Centre (Photo courtesy of Stuart Echols).

52 I am grateful to Professor Stuart P. Echols at Penn State University for his help with this topic and for showing me a rich anthology of striking photographs of these projects, two of which I invoke here. See Stuart Echols and Eliza Pennypacker, "Art for Rain's Sake." *Landscape Architecture*, 96/9 (2006), pp.24–32, and "Learning from Artful Rainwater Design." *Landscape Architecture*, 98/8 (2008), pp.28, 30, 32, 34, 36–9. 2008. Also Eliza Pennypacker, "Perspective: Lessons from a Water Runnel." *Landscape Architecture*, 97/8 (2007), p.36. For other attention to storm drainage systems, see *Fieldwork*, pp.129 ff.
53 Michel Beaujour "Some paradoxes of description", in *Yale French Studies*, 61 (1981), 27–59.

circumstances, when we might be able to see a small garden at a glance, in window boxes, for example, in a Wardian case, or in a dry garden. Even a small garden is liable to change over time, through the seasons, even hour by hour, as a result of light and atmosphere. That a garden and certainly a landscape are not things we can generally "see" at a glance, as when standing before a painting, an architectural facade or a sculpture, makes clear how much time (and whatever weather and atmospheric conditions pertain at a given moment) effects them and affects the visitor. For the essence of landscape is precisely composed of its triple existence in time – our own need to explore a landscape in time, our awareness of how long it has been in existence and how its forms have changed, and its own change over time (hours, months, seasons); also perhaps our own development as responding persons to places through the years that we can get to visit more than once.

When I first visited the gardens of Stowe in Buckingham, with William Gilpin's *Dialogue*[54] in my hand, it required over seven hours to complete the itinerary (I could have read the text in an hour or so); in other visits to Stowe, both the landscape and my own understanding of it have evolved. Moreover, the growth of a garden's natural forms – the shapes of trees above all – subject it to a variety of changes, mostly by its acquiring fullness over the years (thus Alexander Pope's lines – "nature shall make it grow/A work to wonder at perhaps a Stowe"), but also by the decay and death (or disease) of mature trees. But there are also the threats of decay and dissolution. Storms and bad weather can make havoc of garden landscapes; old trees can fail or fall. So landscapes are formed and inevitably reshaped, or deformed, over time, and time takes its place slowly in our imagination as we explore them and continue to think about them afterwards. Time is of the essence in all gardens and landscape and time speaks to us of geology, topographical change and weather.

One final and great example of this collaboration of forces was the design and implementation of Sea Ranch in California, where geologic time, topography, weather/climate and human usage of the site in all its phases collaborated and were made excitingly clear in the design (Figure 2.15). In 1963 Lawrence Halprin among others, especially cultural geographers like Carl Sauer and Richard Reynolds, helped to design a cluster of second homes for people from nearby San Francisco along ten miles of rugged coastline, swept by high winds from the ocean and backed by wooded hillsides.[55] His famous and much published drawing, the "Sea Ranch ecoscore", invoked a huge and clearly grasped diagram in the form of a nautilus shell (itself a natural form): this tracked, from the earliest moments of the earth to the late 20th century, the history of geology, climate, ground cover and

54 I subsequently edited this *Dialogue Upon the Gardens ... at Stowe* by William Gilpin, for the Augustan Reprint Society, 1976.
55 See Halprin, *The Sea Ranch: Diary of an Idea* (Berkeley, CA: Spacemaker Press, 2002), *The Sea Ranch*, ed. Donlyn Lyndon and Jim Alinder (New York: Princeton Architectural Press, 2004), and Kathleen John-Alder, "A field guide to form: Lawrence Halprin's ecological experiment with Sea Ranch", *Landscape Journal* (2013). The "ecoscore" is published, among other places, in *The Sea Ranch, Diary...*, p.18.

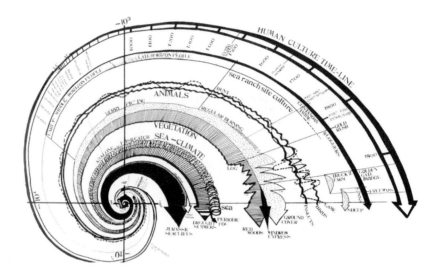

FIGURE 2.15 Lawrence Halprin, "Sea Ranch Ecoscore". (University of Pennsylvania Architectural Archives).

trees, populations and their uses of the site, the advent of gold diggers, sheep farming, truck and farm life, to the means by which, today, people can leave San Francisco and (by the Golden Gate Bridge and freeways) reach Sea Ranch. This understanding of the *long durée* of the site and how its natural energies collaborated with or were abused by earlier human habitations allowed the houses at Sea Ranch to be designed so as to sit easily and happily along the coast, the roofs angled to deflect the Pacific winds and to mimic the trees that had, too, been bent inland, with houses facing the western sun; in short, the opportunity for inhabitants to cultivate an ecological responsibility towards the place. Individual plots are not demarcated, but the land is marked by the hedgerows, a vestige of the previous landscape. Again, we are struck by the simplicity of the design, its visible and understandable forms on the site, and yet the substantial thinking that sustained its complex place in this physical world and promised a newer and more sustainable future. Once again the historical ground is there to be read, immediately and by gradual absorption of the processes that were instrumental to the design of Sea Ranch.

3

EXAMPLES OF HISTORICAL GROUND IN EARLIER LANDSCAPE ARCHITECTURE

Renaissance Rome, Désert de Retz, Les Buttes Chaumont

Gardens have often been established on sites with an earlier history, of one sort or another; the new work can be enhanced by the acknowledgement of an earlier site and its uses. Sometimes the designers knew this and responded, or ignored it accordingly. Sometimes, they may simply be ignorant of what was there, or they may know of archaeological remains, stories and even myths that cling to the place, and relate to them in some fashion. All gardens and landscapes are therefore palimpsests – in practice, or in memory: old "parchments" that have scraped earlier words away to allow new ones to be written there. Some examples from the past will elucidate the varieties of historical performance in garden landscape; they will also show that this approach or strategy is by no means new.

Renaissance villas and gardens in Italy were frequently established on sites above ancient classical gardens; some of these antique sites were known and studied in literature or even known by excavations; but some were just assumed to have been there. In contrast, when the Désert de Retz was created in a forest near Chambourcy, north-west of Paris in the 1780s, nothing was there except the woodland. But its creator, Monsieur de Monville, devised a cluster of buildings that invoked a whole world of past cultures that provided this wooded glade with a history of ancient times and cultures: something like a horizontal as opposed to a vertical palimpsest. Betwixt and between these two approaches to some "historical" ground comes the Parc des Buttes Chaumont in Paris, created by Alphonse Alphand in the 1860s: using a derelict wasteland, where garbage was collected and criminals hanged, he exploited the rocky cliffs and caverns to make a parkland that is now one of the most appreciated sites of Paris. These three examples suggest the range of possibilities for making a historical ground.

If we climb the Palatine Hill from the Roman forum (Figure 3.1), we ascend flights of steps, through a cryptoporticus, pass two elegant 17th-century aviaries, and emerge on the remains of a late 16th- and 17th-century garden, created in the

46 Historical ground in earlier landscape architecture

FIGURE 3.1 Palatine Hill, Rome. (Photo: Anatole Tchkine).

first instance by Cardinal Alessandro Farnese.[1] Below us are the vaults, chambers and garden spaces of ancient Rome, abandoned during the Middle Ages. Early in the 16th century a *vigna* had been established on the hillside, with grottoes and statues, possibly recovered from ancient remains in the site below, or from elsewhere. Further developments occurred in the following century and spread new gardens across the surface of the Palatine Hill. Falda's late 17th-century engraving (Figure 3.2) shows the gardens, with the ascending stairway above the Roman remains at the left of the image and scattered Roman remains below the other slope of the hill. The hill and its Renaissance gardens reflect, as Coffin says, "the splendours of the Roman gardens of antiquity". It is indeed a place where the extent and hugeness of the past is palpable.

Other Renaissance villas and landscapes were similarly – sometimes more hopefully than truly – raised above ancient remains. The Pincian Hill, known since Roman times as the Hill of Gardens, had contained the ancient gardens of Lucullus, Pompey and the poet Sallust.[2] In the late 16th century the Villa Medici was built on the crest of the hillside; while its garden was nothing special, just a series of rectangular beds in a grid pattern, the neighbouring, wooded hillside boasted a Parnassus-like mountain constructed over the remains of an ancient Roman nymphaeum surviving from the Horti Aciliorum.

---

1   These are discussed in detail by David R. Coffin, *Gardens and Gardening in Papal Rome* (Princeton, NJ: Princeton University Press, 1991), pp.69–75. Falda's engraving is illustrated as Figure 56 in Coffin's book.
2   Ibid, pp.215-38.

Historical ground in earlier landscape architecture **47**

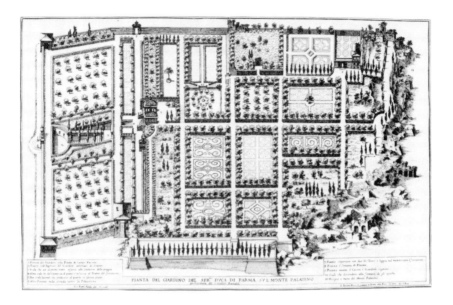

FIGURE 3.2 G.B. Falda, engraving of the gardens on the Palatine Hill, 1670s. (Private collection).

But it was not simply the layering of new gardens on the physical remains of antiquity beneath, but the spread throughout gardens in Rome and the surrounding countryside of ancient sculptures discovered, excavated and displayed (or sometimes copied); this gave to Renaissance gardens the feel, the *color romanus,* of ancient Rome. In his *Unearthing the Past*,[3] Leonard Barkan explores the rich fund of buried sculptures that was unearthed, some Hellenistic, some Roman, and how these treasures were sold off or seized and re-situated in gardens and museums: The Laocoön went to the Vatican Museum, the equestrian statue of Marcus Aurelius was placed on the Capitoline, along with the reclining river gods of Tigris and the Nile. A sculpture of a Lion attacking a Horse is still found in the Palazzo dei Conservatori, but a copy would be found also at the Villa d'Este and even later in the 18th century on the lawn of Rousham in Oxfordshire. In all cases, antique Roman sculpture, or its copies, offered memories of the past to the respective landscapes, for it lent a proper *romanitas* to a new garden or landscape. What had been unearthed, became visible now on the surface.

3 *Unearthing the Past: Archaeology and Aesthetics in the Making of Renaissance Culture* (New Haven, CT: Yale University Press, 1999). But the fundamental source for this is Rodolfo Lanciani, *Storia degli scavi di Roma* (1899), and the modern commentary on it by David E. Karmon, *The Ruin of the Eternal City: Antiquity and Preservation in Renaissance Rome* (New York: Oxford University Press, 2012). On the English fascination for and partial knowledge of ancient Roman villas and gardens, see my *Garden and Grove: The Italian Renaissance Garden in the English Imagination 1600–1750* (London: Dent, 1986), Chapter 2.

48 Historical ground in earlier landscape architecture

To see the long traditions of a completely invented history or what might be called a memorial narrative, we might turn to one of the most mysterious and creative instances of landscape architecture – the Désert de Retz (Figure 3.3) – to the north-west of Paris. Created by a certain Monsieur de Monville in the 1780s (a period of great scientific and philosophical Enlightenment), he proposed assembling the complete sum "de la connaissance et des curiosités de l'homme du XVIIIe siècle" ("the 18th-century man's knowledge and curiosities [meaning things that we should be curious about]"). So he gathered a collection of buildings from many civilizations – the remains of a gothic church, an Egyptian Pyramid, an antique Theatre or rostrum, a Turkish tent (now restored), a Chinese House (long since destroyed), a ruined classical temple dedicated to Pan and – most notably – a huge and supposedly "destroyed" column, that (because never "completed") would have been a vast and imposing structure 120 metres high! He also established a horticultural ground at the edge of the clearing, a long-standing tradition, but one that had acquired special significance during the Enlightenment, where the intensive study of plants was designed to improve scientific knowledge and therefore advance the progress of mankind.

Such fragments of global culture made clear that visitors needed to respond to these human recollections of the *longue durée* of civilizations.[4] The Désert suggests that de Monville deliberately conceived of the place "to satisfy [a] free play of consciousness and retrospective imaginations.... the garden's potential to carve out a [historical] space amidst the contemporary urban theatre...".[5] Yet this astonishing creation needs more than such general reflections. The poet and critic, Yves Bonnefoy, published an essay in 1993 that sought a more acute appraisal of the site.[6] He proposed that de Monville had gathered recollections of many historical civilizations – along with a horticultural garden – that would be the epitome of all cultures and religions, or maybe a meditation on the decadence and imminent end of all human achievements. On the eve of the French Revolution, says Bonnefoy, the Désert de Retz became a ground where we could contemplate history in all its grandeur and its decadence – *désert* here signals a place of meditation (that sort of retreat, not a wilderness). For in this place our attention was directed to what was known from all the regions and cultures of the earth: in each case, with each structure, we were confronted with a true place ("*lieu*"), or what Bonnefoy calls a gravitational field ("un champ de gravitation"). Instead of a series of abstract ideas, here was a real object that implied the location where ideas and life were actually focused. But these creations in the valley of de Retz are, however, wholly fictive, an invented or fabricated ground (the church ruin is "real"). This is what makes an act of historical reconstruction, in the words of Bonnefoy, an "authentic modernity".

4   Michel Baridon, *Les Jardins: Paysagistes-jardiniers-poètes* (Paris: Laffont, 1998), pp.832–5.
5   Sébastien Marot, *Sub-Urbanism and the Art of Memory* (London: Architectural Association, 2003), p.32. I have added "historical" to underline the thrust of his remark.
6   "Le Désert de Retz et l'expérience du lieu", in his collection *Le nuage rouge* (Paris: Editions du Mercure de France, 1999), pp.367–82.

Historical ground in earlier landscape architecture **49**

FIGURE 3.3 Désert de Retz, near Chambourcy, France. (a) Chinese House (demolished), engraving from late 18th century (private collection), and (b) the "Ruined Column", with theatre fragment in the foreground.

50 Historical ground in earlier landscape architecture

A similar manoeuvre works at the Parc des Buttes Chaumont, where 19th-century technology created a landscape that survives as a modern parkland that yet gives the impression of being a much more ancient place. The site was a wasteland and quarry, where garbage was piled high, and criminals hanged; a railway line for the Chemin de Fer de Ceinture ran alongside it. Alphand transformed the site by augmenting the cliffs and the caverns, adding a modern suspension bridge designed by Eiffel (Figure 3.4), and topping its highest cliff with the replica of an ancient classical temple. What has been called "engineered picturesque"[7] overlaid new materials and techniques on the carefully configured landform, which were themselves the result of new topographical surveys that Alphand published in *Les Promenades de Paris*. Both the modern mapping, for which France had became a leader by the 18th century, and the inventive use of concrete to simulate rocks, geological conditions and authentic looking stalactites made this ground strikingly new and at the same time curiously old: the "antique" tempietto was concrete, as were the retaining walls of the railway cutting, and the handrails and stairs throughout the park were reinforced concrete, but looked like wooden logs (many still survive; see Figure 3.4). Its allusions to some historical past – wooden fencing, memories of the gibbets, the sublime cliffs of Normandy on which the caves and stalactites were modelled, an antique temple with intimations of some sacred past – coexisted with masses of new soil and planting, a modern railway line and a suspension bridge. This "reinvention of nature"[8] got a mixed response: William Robinson disliked the "plasterwork" of the cliff, but found the grotto "well formed and striking", though he demurred about its suitability for "a public garden".[9] It was altogether a strange and wondrous amalgam of old and new materials, found and invented forms and recollections, which the new science of photography would also seek out as a rich subject to depict.

So, three sites: one based consciously and physically upon ancient gardens, one wholly fabricated, and another that plays with both of these approaches. Two of these, in Rome and in Paris, contrive a palimpsestial site, a new one overlaid upon the old. The third in the forests outside Paris does not layer its ground, but – like Renaissance Rome with its newly unearthed and variously displayed antique sculptures – positions a series of historical structures, each of which commands some recognition of the place and the different cultures from which the item was supposedly derived.

What has been called a "double historicity" is at work in all three sites, irrespective of the different means by which they were devised or envisaged. We know they are fabricated in a present, or maybe in the recent past, but we "value

7 Ann Komara, "Concrete and the Engineered Picturesque: The Parc des Buttes Chaumont (Paris, 1867)", *Journal of Architectural Education* (2004), p.5. See also "Measure and Map: Alphand's contours of construction at the Parc des Buttes Chaumont, Paris 1967", *Landscape Journal*, 28 (2009), pp.22–39.
8 Nicholas Green, *The Spectacle of Nature: Landscape and Bourgeois Culture in 19th-century France* (Manchester, UK: Manchester University Press, 1990), p.69.
9 *The Parks, Promenades and Gardens of Paris* (London, 1869), pp.62 and 67.

Historical ground in earlier landscape architecture 51

FIGURE 3.4 Parc des Buttes Chaumont, Paris, France. (a) The suspension bridge by Eiffel, and (b) one of the many fences cast in concrete in imitation of tree trunks (Photo: Emily T. Cooperman).

52 Historical ground in earlier landscape architecture

them and use them as if they were old things".[10] What might seem more apt to call them fakes, like de Monville's different structures, is better understood as an "anachronism"; old things or places have a "referential authority to auratic originals deemed even more ancient" than modern structures, though modern they are.

So, these past examples suggest a variety of ways in which gardens and parks imitate, literally or metaphorically, a palimpsest, as opposed to an attempt to just cover up one that is deemed old-fashioned or maybe too expensive to maintain. So it is important to ask how an earlier site can be made visible and how it can tell its tale. The three sites respond in different ways to those challenges: seeing actual topographical or archaeological remains, registering recreated images of some historical past, in each case combined with an inventive imagination. The next three chapters will set out the varieties of contemporary historical ground that have been projected or established by exploring that same variety of approaches.

10 Hal Foster in the *Times Literary Supplement* of 8 November 2012, p. 12, citing in particular Alexander Nagel and Christopher Wood, *Anachronic Renaissance* (New York: Zone Books, 2010).

4

FIVE PARISIAN SITES

A scale of contemporary invention and intervention

To gauge the range of how history is made visible on contemporary sites – whether "found", fractured (i.e. fragments only), or invented history, there are five gardens or parks on Paris where this scale can be perfectly exhibited and analysed: Parcs André Citroën and Bercy; Jardin (now Parc) Diderot; Jardin Atlantique; and the Jardins d'Eole (as it is now called). These sites are by now well known to students of modern design (except perhaps the last), but have not been explored as historical ground: they can profitably be examined as sites that range from ones with a record of minimal history, to those where remnants of historical buildings or conspicuous topography are exposed and augmented, and finally to a wholly invented or anachronic site, where "history" finds a means of creating a wholly new, but plausible, memory of an old or distant one. These five sites will establish the range and variety of historical reference, a scale for other contemporary landscapes in the two, more lengthy, chapters that follow.

Parc André Citroën (Figure 4.1) now occupies the former Citroën factory and HQ along the River Seine. It gives it name, obviously, to the park, and – if you can find it on one of the terraces – there is a small and inscribed bust of Monsieur Citroën; though one might have thought that a model of a *deux chevaux* automobile on a pedestal might recall more of what at one time for many people the Citroën car manufactory was known for. The park occupies ground between new apartment blocks and is serviced by two metro stations outside and at opposite ends of the park; these are connected by the straight path that crosses the parkland obliquely and is the only indication of a street that once was there: this obvious path, slightly eccentric in French garden terms – namely a diagonal line across a small segment of the central lawn (a *tapis vert),* is really the only hint of the layout of the earlier urban area. The new *quartier* has a bistro at one end, and the surroundings of park and garden merge imperceptibly with the new area and streetscape. The park itself is elaborate, but its conservatories, nymphaea or grottoes,

54 Five Parisian sites

FIGURE 4.1 Parc André Citroën, Paris. Plan of the park and inset of the bust of Monsieur Citroën.

fountains, and a variety of small gardens (a black garden, a white garden, etc.) do not signal any obvious older ground: it is a new and much used parkland, and it is doubtful whether the elaborate forms and elements, especially those that are highlighted in six serial gardens along the northern side, can remind one very forcibly of earlier gardens and landscape materials, though they are clearly derived from traditions of garden-making.

Opposite the bistro is a children's playground bordered at one end by a row of granite blocks, clearly marked by their extraction from a quarry, out of which come spouts of water. *Sources* of rivers were historically marked by river gods, themselves a formal means in ancient Rome and the Renaissance of signalling springs in the landscape; but here it is just the geological blocks and jets that suggest, if at all, the sources of rivers and streams. The slope between the two large conservatories that overlook the large lawn has fountains, jets controlled by computers that rise and fall randomly, and delight the children who play among them. On one side of the open lawn are a series of concrete grottoes, not particularly successful, indeed rather forlorn; but these are also supposedly hints of earlier and less austere forms of garden nymphaea or grottoes.

On the opposite, north-east edge of the gardens is a much more inviting sequence of six small greenhouses or conservatories, reached on an elevated pathway, in front of each is an oblong, so-called "serial" garden that descends towards the central lawn. These are each different in layout and purport to display and ask us to meditate upon a whole conspectus of ideas. That they have some historical resonance seems clear, but the clues and suggestions are somewhat

Five Parisian sites **55**

obscure, and frankly leave me and other commentators at a loss.[1] The six gardens have been termed "pedagogical", for plaques alongside each space denominate symbolic associations, metals and dominant colours; these "heavy-handed" notations can readily be left alone, it being better, as Michel Racine notes, "aller aux plaisirs des changements d'ambiances" ("go to visit the pleasures of the changes in the surroundings"); namely the other gardens, the small conservatories and parkscape generally. So Parc Citroën is a place that has some historical triggers if you want to respond to them, but nothing that compels much attention to the history of this particular ground.

Parc Bercy, at the opposite end of Paris, is also a new park created on the site of the *Dépôts des Vins*, the former storage and shipping facility for French wines. Much of the site makes no attempt to recognize its previous existence, though like everything in this area of Paris this area had a long and rich tradition of mansions and river usage along the River Seine. The park (Figure 4.2) has gardens of different kinds and layouts, a small vineyard that recalls the wine industry, lawns (a somewhat rare event in Parisian parks for people may walk on them, and a notice even encourages them to do so), elements that are supposed to signal the different seasons (not very effective or clear) and others that signal, again somewhat obliquely, the four elements (for example, a brick chimney evokes Fire), a series of small beds in a *potager*, and a supposedly romantic or "picturesque" garden with ponds and a snail-mound. Like Citroën, it can, I suppose, if one is so-minded, make one think of earlier garden forms; its older trees recall 19th-century Parisian parks and the various sections evoke distinct garden typologies. It is a space that I like and find intriguing, not least for its dedication to different layouts, as the plan on display makes very clear. Of course, many other gardens invoke the past deliberately or by allusion, from Renaissance gardens' recall of antique gardens and villas to the various imitations of earlier cultural forms during the picturesque movement (Gothic, Chinese, or American follies). But at Bercy, and indeed at Citroën, there is little incentive here to probe that gardenist past; but at least one commentator has shown that research on Bercy can foreground elements of the past that visitors might miss.[2]

Created by a team led by the urbanist architect Bernard Huet, the Bercy project was originally called a "Jardin de la Mémoire", a name that no longer survives on the site or in most visitors' consciousness. There are, certainly, items in the parkland that might trigger memories: a former gardener's house, a house of a former wine-merchant by the lake in the romantic sector, former buildings that housed storage

---

1   Michel Racine, *Jardins en France* (Arles, France: Actes Sud, 1997), p.202, where he notices that is it not really necessary to probe the pedagogical themes of these six gardens!

2   Amanda Shoaf Vincent, "Bercy's Jardin de la Mémoire: Ruin, allegory, memory", *Landscape Journal*, 29/1 (2010), pp. 36–51. The article contains a cluster of other commentaries on Parc Bercy, but in her effort to make the history or "memory" available she invokes Walter Benjamin's notions of allegory in *The Origins of German Tragic Drama*, surely a rather desperate move to give the park intellectual substance.

56 Five Parisian sites

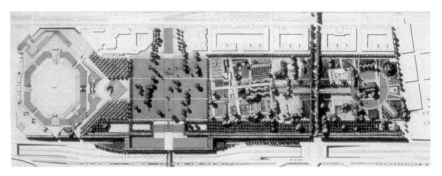

FIGURE 4.2 Parc Bercy, Paris. Plan of the site.

areas for the aging of wine, ruined bits of the Petit Chateau de Bercy (somewhat hidden away in a corner), a range of what look like wine cellars, and a virtuoso display of different garden types. But the original Bercy chateau has gone, as have the commercial and port areas along the Seine that once were in what is now the 12th *arrondissement*; nor are the original uses of such buildings as survive made clear for today's visitors.

However, one aspect of the former *Dépôts des Vins* clearly survives, a slight but telling remnant. Once upon a time huge wine casks were moved on rails around the site, and some of these rails are still embedded in the pavements. These old pavements are also lower than the central, modern walkway and on some of the subsidiary lower garden paths have been formed around the former rail tracks; as these are set at an angle to the path, they are more visible. Some years ago there was one of these huge casks on a trolley at the far end of the park (though when last I was there it had gone), and this suddenly made clearer what a vast enterprise had been here originally.

One other element lingers: a line of arcades – what one might assume is a fragment of where wine would have been stored in vaults – is established along the northern side of the park; it reminds me somewhat of a range of dispossessed cathedral quire stalls – so we have to think hard to recall wine cellars. In fact, they are not related to the site at all, since the arcade has been moved here after the demolition of the Saint-Germaine Market.[3] But otherwise it is in the cafés and stores at the eastern end of the park, in a set of restored and augmented warehouses, that we might recall the original uses of the site: in this new *quartier*, visiting tourists can shop and others can drink their wine in the so-called Cour Saint-Emilion.

If rail tracks, vaults and huge wine casks signal a lost area of old Paris in the east, beyond the western end of Paris in the Défense area, among the modern towers, the

---

3   I owe this information to Vincent, ibid, p.42. Since the Bercy site and the Saint Germaine market were owned by the same entity, the financial department of the Ville de Paris, it is clear that these arcades might have transferred to Bercy from the market.

escalators, stairways and labyrinthine office and apartments blocks, is a small garden (now rechristened a park) where the topography is startling; this invented urban space brings to life those who work or live in the surrounding buildings. The Défense occupies, of course, a huge hillside, but the scale of the main approach to the *Arche* with its vast opening dwarfs our sense of the ascent. But the scale of the Jardin (now Parc) Diderot (Figure 4.3) is small and set on a considerable slope that is further accentuated by a rushing stream (of recycled water). In the rushing water are a series of thin slabs of rocks, set lengthwise in the flow, and this exaggerates the pace and agitation of the water as well as underlining the slope of the garden space. Parallel with the water course are four hedges, that sweep down the hillside and seem (another Genette pun) like green escalators, of a piece, wittily, with the real escalators up and down which one moves in the main Défense plaza. The difficulty of discovering this hidden space makes its appearance in this urban wilderness the more surprising and satisfying (hint: make for Zone 3 and consult a posted map there).

If Diderot utilizes the given topography, though exaggerating the slope with water effects and with obviously artificial rocks, the Jardin Atlantique is wholly factitious. My students, seeing it presented in a PowerPoint display in some classroom, think it is corny and simply theatrical; on site, when I'm lucky enough to be there with some of them, they are more reassured, if not readily impressed.

Jardin Atlantique is many things. It is a garden. But it is also a waiting room, suspended above the departure platforms of the Gare Montparnasse, for those waiting to board the TGV trains that depart for the Atlantic coast. It is also a

FIGURE 4.3 Parc (formerly Jardin) Diderot, La Défense, Paris. (Photo: Emily T. Cooperman).

playground – for kids on model galleons and bouncing dolphins, or for adults on the blue tennis courts that lie to one side of the garden. It is a weather station, for at the centre of the garden is a meteorological station, with wind and rain gauges. It is also a park for the surrounding high-rise apartments. Its central *allée*, the Allée Du Capitaine-Dronne, commemorates the re-taking of Paris by French troops in 1945. So the Jardin Atlantique is a palimpsest in its provision of so many amenities, but also it is literally layered about the railway station. But it is wholly fake. There was no garden or park here before (indeed this area of Paris lacks such an amenity, which is maybe why it is appreciated now by local inhabitants), and the Atlantic is far, far away. In fact, the Atlantic coast is wholly displaced into this Parisian garden. Nor is it particularly easy to find: we can climb some obscure stairs from inside the station, passing on the way a most uninviting and gloomy waiting room; or we can take an elevator from a side street outside (if it is working) and then cross a gangway into the garden.

The platform on which the garden rests cannot sustain much planting, and vents in the floor throughout the garden emit the subdued noises and rumblings of the TGVs below. The garden contains a boardwalk, slightly tilting towards the "ocean", and across the grass a series of coloured waves "lap" against it (this is surely a Genette-like parody of the waves that come "ashore" on the other side of the Atlantic, at Copacabana Beach in Rio de Janeiro by Roberto Burle Marx); on the boards, or maybe "beach", people can recline and sunbathe (Figure 4.4). There is some unmistakable seaside planting, low and resistant to the sea (or

FIGURE 4.4 Jardin Atlantique, Gare Montparnasse, Paris. The "boardwalk" and the "waves". (Photo: Emily T. Cooperman).

urban) air. Across from the boardwalk are two "caves" in the "cliffs" (Figure 4.5), and behind them, on a raised promenade, there is a path behind the "cliffs", which might be found along the actual coast. Seeing the "caves" now from the rear, as one walks the cliff path, the garden's scenography is most apparent, if it had not been before. Regarded now from this perspective, the "caves" are thin slabs of rock or marble, positioned like theatrical flats and supported by struts in the rear. Seeing these, it is not unlike those moments in Renaissance garden grottoes where visitors, intrigued, even convinced, by the hydraulic performances, the moving statues and the music, could visit behind the "scenes" and see how all the machinery worked. John Evelyn, for one, was delighted by these inventions, and by no means disappointed when he came "out front" and saw the performances once again.

The idea of the Jardin Atlantique is to be the place *from where* you go to the seaside, so it provides you with a repertoire, or an epitome, of the Atlantic coast – caves, cliffs, boardwalks, waves, playgrounds – that you would find when you get there. If you are unlucky and are not bound for the coast, then you have to put up with the pretence; you 'do' the seaside in the midst of Paris. If in fact you *are* going there, you of course reach the real thing in a couple of hours. I am always reminded of the early scene in Jacques Tati's film, *Les Vacances de Monsieur Hulot*: the hubbub at the old station, where the inaudible loudspeakers are sending people backwards and forwards, down and up the stairways onto different platforms, with their buckets and spades, tennis rackets, and the other paraphernalia of the seaside, to

FIGURE 4.5 Jardin Atlantique, Gare Montparnasse, Paris. The "caves" in the "cliff".
(Photo: Emily T. Cooperman).

60 Five Parisian sites

catch the train, which eventually appears on yet another platform; Hulot, meanwhile, takes his rickety Citroën car through the countryside.

The English critic, Samuel Taylor Coleridge, famously distinguished between the creations of the imagination and the world of fancy.[4] I assume that it is what my sceptical students could refer to when seeing the Jardin Atlantique: that it is merely fanciful, and by no means a work of the imagination. They have a point, but what they miss perhaps is the humorous play with this site, as few landscape architects relish any taste for the absurd or surreal; also they forget that so many gardens in the past have been theatrical experiences, often as fabricated as this one is. But the designers of this one, Christine and Michel Péna,[5] suggest that they do have a sense of play. The fancy, Coleridge thought, was fixed and definite, a mode of ordinary memory, with no other counters for the mind to play with. Imagination, on the other hand, "dissolves, diffuses, dissipates, in order to recreate"; it idealizes and unifies, and it is essentially "vital". I do not think Coleridge would be so impressed with this pleasure garden as to think it a place of the imagination like Kubla Khan decreed at Xanadu ("a stately pleasure dome … Where Alph, the sacred river, ran / Through caverns measureless to man / Down to a sunless sea…"). Yet the Paris garden is vital, takes a certain pleasure in its fabrication, indulges those who fancy (*sic*) the chance of getting to the Atlantic coast, which they can begin to imagine, and affords its visitors or neighbours a suitably theatrical show, a stage in which they can play at the seaside.

A fifth site appeals clearly to its immediate past, though with less imaginative excitement. What was first called the Parc de la Cour du Maroc,[6] a reference to the Moroccan immigrants who lived thereabouts, is now known as the Jardins d'Eole[7] (Figure 4.6). The park was formed after insistent demands over many years by the local Association des Jardins d'Eole, which established its own newsletter, *Un Bout du Monde*, to promote it; the newsletter (http://kelkit.perso.neuf.fr) makes clear how much the history of this ground was a result of local activism to preserve not only the site itself from development but the "spirit" of the inhabitants who would use it. This park or garden outside the Gares du Nord and de l'Est in the 19th arrondissement fills the spaces, left by the railroads sidings and marshalling or switching yards, with narrow lawns, a slim canal and paths that also take their

---

4   This brief explanation is set out in his 1812 *Biographia Literaria*, 2 vols, ed. J. Shawcross (Oxford, UK: Oxford University Press, 1907), a dense and difficult work: but the distinction used here has a certain simplicity: see op. cit., I, 202.

5   Their work is featured in *Pour une troisième nature* (Paris: ICI Interface, 2010), with bilingual texts. For this design, pp.92–7.

6   Peter Reed, *Groundswell: Constructing the Contemporary Landscape* (New York: Museum of Modern Art, 2005), pp. 138–43.

7   I had always thought, and this notion was even confirmed by others, that this garden was dedicated to Aeolus, God of the winds. It is in fact named after the rail line known as "Est-Ouest Liaison Express (EOLE)"; for which see Malcolm Woollen, "Les Jardins d'Eole: Extending the picturesque", *Studies in the History of Gardens and Designed Landscapes* (2013/4), to whose essay I am indebted here.

FIGURE 4.6 Les Jardins d'Eole, Paris. (Photo: Emily T. Cooperman).

direction from the long latitudinal space. The newest of the Parisian parks acknowledges the shape of the original industrial area: besides accentuating that space by accepting the long narrow site along the lines of the former tracks, the lower level is paralleled with a raised steel footbridge. From above visitors get a clear sense of both the shape of the park on the east and a view of the still existing and functioning railway lines leaving the two stations to the west; below, pedestrians can also glimpse the rail yard through slots in the red wall designed by Carmen Perrin, or turn away to contemplate the park itself. There is also a gravel garden, referencing the ballast from abandoned railways, which will promote hardy wild flowers and require minimal care. The open space is much needed and will provide an open area for a largely immigrant neighbourhood, with play areas, sporting facilities, spots of quiet seclusion and plots for growing vegetables.

These five sites provide a useful scale for understanding historical ground. Citroën barely registers the former HQ and factory. Bercy make some gestures towards the former wine depot ("a creative response to a historical site"[8] – though with more emphasis on creation than history); otherwise there is little attempt to recall the past. But both have created parks that enhance the city of Paris in the tradition of older landscape designers in the Haussmann years, and that is an important historical gesture. Parc Diderot utilizes its hillside, and with the augmentation of its slope makes the topography clear; it is at all times a lively and fun

8 Vincent, op. cit., p.36.

62 Five Parisian sites

interlude in the dreary world of the Défense. The Atlantique covers over and conceals the departure platforms of a major train station and on it invents a ground where no garden could conceivably have been – in fact two "grounds": a distant seaside destination, and the *allée* that marks a major recovery of the French city at the end of the German occupation in 1945. Eole does not bother to hide the former train tracks, but exploits them for its own stretch of open space beside the still surviving railway network. These different Parisian sites suggest the range of how contemporary designers have approached the two fundamental approaches to historical ground, which the next two chapters explore: first, histories found and exploited on sites, then those invented for them.

5

HISTORY FOUND AND EXPLOITED IN A SPECIFIC PLACE

"The past is never dead. It's not even past"

(William Faulkner)

Memorials

Memorials are an obvious place to start, though many do not figure as landscaped places. Some memorials record and/or honour events or people in the place where they occurred. Some record events in a different place, or far away – any Vietnam Memorial, for example, outside Vietnam itself. All memorials recall some person or persons, some event or some cause, for those who are able or wish to recall them, but not for those for whom that bit of the past has been forgotten; they have, if at all, to make to make an effort to learn about it. There is a memorial for the Camel Corps on the Thames Embankment near Charing Cross, but I'd be surprised how many people these days actually served in or know what the Camel Corps was. There is also, among other items there, a statue of Gilbert (or is it Sullivan?); but as we can listen to their operas, that memorial has less saliency.

These days there are memorials everywhere, so much so that this has been termed a "Memorial Mania".[1] A notable example is cited by Erika Doss, who explains that, after Daniel Libeskind designed a fine addition for the Denver Art Museum, its staff had to determine what to do with an outdoor space, for which

---

1 Erika Doss, *Memorial Mania: Public Feeling in America* (Chicago, IL: University of Chicago Press, 2010). Her example is from p.7. Other references will be in the text. The literature is large: see especially Julian Bonder, "On memory, trauma, public space, monuments and memorials', *Places*, 21/1 (2009), pp.62–9; Edward W. Said, "Invention, memory, and place", *Critical Inquiry*, 26/2 (2000), pp.175–92; *Monuments and Memory, Made and Unmade,* ed. Robert S. Nelson and Margaret Olin (Chicago, IL: Chicago University Press, 2003); Jas Elsner, "Iconoclasm and the Preservation of Memory", in ibid.

64 History found and exploited in a specific place

Libeskind immediately proposed a "memorial"; to which the staff responded with "Memorial to what?" We need to parse this profusion to yield some interesting aspects of historical ground, which is otherwise cluttered with distractions. Too many memorials address events or causes that have no specific topographical site, or are for people whose memories are not related to that place. This is not to say, some crazy examples aside, that these causes and people are unimportant, but what properly concerns historical ground is whether a memorial honours a site where the disaster occurred. All memorials recall us to the "signs of the passage of time as well as enthusiasm for the new",[2] but especially so in a specific place. They are places or "sites where memory [sc. history] is crystallized".[3]

There are many memorials now of the holocaust, events that we do well to recall and lament; but some have no reason for being situated where they are (and many, too, have a less than impressive design, which probably matters if the designer needs to remind us of its subject).[4] On the other hand, it is hard to see how any intervention by a designer can or should do anything to "improve", let alone – what is the word? – embellish or make more visible and known any of the sites where these atrocities, on such a large scale, took place. Better the mute emptiness, surely, than any attempt to "*reinfuse* the sites with a sense of their historical past".[5] Yet we also need to engage with what Pierre Nora, also cited by Young, calls "the will to remember". We cannot forget, and must be made *not* to forget, especially in the places where these events took place.

Yet even "mute emptiness" has been at issue throughout the years since the extermination camps were liberated in 1945. The narrative of how to commemorate the sites at Majdanek and Auschwitz has been well rehearsed by James Young and will not be repeated here. But the energies of the memorialists has tended to neglect how the Polish landscape itself is treated; "official memories" have had to compete with rival versions of how the past can be commemorated on the site, and whether a memorial can be confined to the physical spaces of the landscape alone. There are not only the ruined buildings, some gas chambers dynamited by the Germans themselves at Birkenau (which has more recently raised the issue of to what extent, and how, can ruins be "preserved", and how does one record that piece of German destruction), but the "museological remnants" (displays of prisoners' clothing, bins of shoes, suitcases, etc.) and the various pavilions dedicated to Jews of non-Polish nations. These landscapes today involve both extensive and palimpsestial areas that include the ruins, barracks converted to

2   Introduction to *Monuments and Memory…*, p.2.
3   Pierre Nora, *Realms of Memory: Rethinking the French Past*, trans. Arthur Goldhammer, 3 vols (NY: Columbia University Press, 1996–98), I, p.1.
4   James E. Young, *The Texture of Memory: Holocaust Memorials and Meaning* (New Haven, CT: Yale University Press, 1993), to whose careful narrative (given that I have not been to these sites) I am much indebted. I have also consulted *How the Holocaust Looks Now*, eds. Martin L. Davies and Claus-Christian W. Szejnmann (New York: Palgrave Macmillan, 2007).
5   Young, p.119, my italics.

exhibition spaces, rail lines, the full grown trees that the Germans planted at Auschwitz to screen the camp itself, but also the farmers who now work the land, and young people who fish the adjacent pond beside the crematoria, or the kids who ride their bicycles through the birch groves. These "local citizens", says Young, become part of "our memory here, reinforcing our own prejudices, perhaps, feeding our disgust" (p.144). The potential for a "future" can collide with our prejudices and its recall of the past.

To attempt to commemorate that past, an international design competition was held in 1957, chaired by the distinguished sculptor Henry Moore, whose work has enhanced landscapes everywhere and whose sculptures inserted into the land draw us into responding to their sites.[6] Of over 400 submissions from 36 countries, seven teams were selected and asked to visit the landscape at Auschwitz. In his presentation of the entries, Moore lamented that no "very great sculptor – a new Michaelangelo [n]or a new Rodin" had emerged to satisfy the jurors. Three groups of designers were eventually asked to work together to combine their projects into one – some have dominated the place with either abstract or over-realistic sculptures, some had responded feelingly to the landscape itself, acknowledging the emptiness of the site or excavating a deep, grave-like basin surrounded by canals. All designers were committed to the competition's requirement that the remnants of the site not be altered. Once the final monument was chosen, further adjustments had to be made, even to the finished design as it was being installed, by making its sculptural additions more abstract; this was largely a result of the need to respond to the tensions between commemorating the Jews as well as the communists and political prisoners, whom the German had also eliminated. Inscriptions at Birkenau had also to be erased, since an original claim of 4 million victims proved to be unfounded.

A "monument to crime and ugliness, to murder and to horror" (in Henry Moore's words) is virtually beyond the reach of those many who suffered and also of those who, born since these events, could comprehend it fully. Plural memories inscribe themselves on the landscape: the Jews who originally were forced to build the camp at Auschwitz, the village of Brzezinka raised by Germans in order to build the barracks there. Perhaps it can only be, as Young admits, the "physical topography supplemented by historical significance" that manages to be a sufficient monument, Therefore it does seem that one of the more resonant monuments, this time at Majdanek, responds both to the land and with a sufficiently abstract memorial (Figure 5.1): the approach to Wiktor Tolkin's sculpture, dedicated in 1969, leads us up from a symbolic valley of death past jagged rocks that guard the steps, at the top of which we are overwhelmed by the lintel of Tolkin's threatening work; looking between its twin supports, and almost a mile away, is the dome over the mausoleum of ashes at the gas chambers, and crematorium with its chimney.

---

6   I am thinking here of how his sculptures help us to see a site afresh, after that memorable poem by Wallace Stevens, "The Anecdote of a Jar", where a "jar" on a hill in Tennessee helps us envision the landscape anew.

FIGURE 5.1 The memorial by Wiktor Tolkin at Majdanek, Poland. Reprinted from James E. Young, The Texture of Memory (New Haven, CT: Yale University Press). (Courtesy of the author).

Here it is indeed the landscape as a whole that may speak sufficiently to our sadness, awe and our acknowledgement of the "historical significance" of the holocaust.

Erika Doss argues that American memorials are "archives of public affect", a term derived from the Latin *affectus*, meaning "passion" and "disposition of mind", with the additional sense of "to afflict" or "to touch" (p.15). Historical sites that concern us in this discussion may well affect and afflict, but they also do so in ways that foreground why the memorial should be in a specific place. The various memorials for 9/11 are fitting examples of a true historical ground, as are battlefields.

The World Trade Center has been the site of divisive and bitter quarrels among those immediately concerned with this commemoration of the attack on 9/11, notably how its designers should respond to this memorialization and how they were required to redefine it in response to those arguments. So, too, was the Memorial for Flight 93 at Shanksville, Pennsylvania. What is in question here, in all these designs and in the arguments that convulsed them, is how the place itself – the sites of the terrorist attacks – becomes part of the memorial vocabulary. Those two sites, as well as the Pentagon Memorial, vary considerably in how historical ground is constituted.

At the Pentagon, the very building itself, as the seat of the US military, and the area where the plane crashed immediately before it, are the *site*: yet the design by Julie Beckman and Keith Kaseman, does little to record the *place*, other than to situate it in front of the building that was attacked, rather attending wholly to its victims on the plane and from the Pentagon itself: the strange benches and inscribed names do not make much sense of why this memorial is there and have little real relationship to the damaged and now repaired building. One is struck rather by the strange immodesty of the design[7]. At Shanksville, on the other hand (once the unseemly anger at the first design was adjusted, even though the outrage seemed beside the point) the Field of Honor, designed by Paul Murdoch, has a ceremonial gateway that leads to a walled and "sacred" space that marks the final resting place of the passengers and crew. Its pastoral setting and the Tower of Voices, with wind chimes, do something to give the place itself a role in the memorial.

It is in New York that the place itself seems to achieve the best role among these 9/11 memorials. Despite some calls to leave the remains as a ruin (though ruins are not a resonant image in the national character of America[8]), what did get designed has two elements that draw attention to the site and do much to triumph over the endless quarrels about how the event should be commemorated: the pools and the grove of trees, in the design called "Reflecting Absence" by Michel Arad, joined later by the landscape architect, Peter Walker (Figure 5.2). Despite calls to build bigger and taller towers on the same ground, the two designers determined that pools on the footprints of the original buildings would be the memorial, and it surely succeeds: their emptiness is a register of what was there, their watery depths are something that each visitor, whether bereaved family members or tourists, must fathom in his or her own way; while the noise of the water drowns out external noises and shuts everyone up in his or her own memory or reflections. A grove of trees (Swamp White Oak and Sweet Gum) has no local reason for being there, but

7   For a lengthy assessment of the Pentagon memorial, not in the end very affirmative, see Victoria Carchidi, "Struggling with terror; the Pentagon memorial", *Studies in the History of Gardens and Designed Landscapes,* 30/3, pp.193–207, with many illustrations.

8   As J.B. Jackson argued in *The Necessity for Ruins and Other Topics* (1980), quoted by Doss, op. cit., p.173. John Ruskin also, as quoted above in Chapter Two, opined that ruins were an "instinct ... which ... can hardly be felt in America", *The Library Edition of the Works of John Ruskin*, vol. V, p.369.

FIGURE 5.2 The 9/11 Memorial, New York. (Courtesy of PWP Architecture).

groves of trees have been sacred since Greek times[9], and greenness and beauty in the midst of lower Manhattan are to be relished and seem a legitimate promise of long-term healing.

That those who lost their lives are commemorated is clearly important for all their relatives. But for others not personally touched by the site, indeed the many others not directly affected, it is the sheer litany of names, the catalogue of so many victims, that holds us, the more so if one is not searching for a particular name but struck simply by the multitude of the victims (the same is true for Maya Lin's Vietnam Memorial in Washington, DC). Those intimately concerned with the loss of loved ones or colleagues will doubtless want more: the adjacent Memorial Museum at 9/11 in New York tries to supply this, as do the rather clumsy figurative group of soldiers fighting in Vietnam near the Washington Vietnam Memorial, which may satisfy those for whom Lin's black walls and eloquent understatement of a terrible war do not appeal. Yet those different adjuncts do not make the *place* itself resonant or compelling. Though, if we respond to it, then the place on the Washington Mall *does* itself become part of an invented and truly historical ground.

European memorials, in Berlin and in Amsterdam, seem to negotiate the past and make the ground itself sensible of its history and yet also establish them as places for the future; if not "enthusiasm for the new", at least a promise of healing. A cargo plane, with a crew of four, crashed into an apartment building in

9   See Patrick Bowe, "The sacred groves of Ancient Greece", *Studies in the History of Gardens and Designed Landscapes,* 29/4 (2009), pp.235–45.

History found and exploited in a specific place **69**

Amsterdam on 4th October 1992, where it killed 47 people and injured others; as always in these circumstances a memorial involved delicate negotiations with the bereaved and local authorities, but also with the place itself: Georges Descombes, working with the Dutch architect Herman Hertzberger, seems to have succeeded with the Bijlmer Memorial.[10] A solitary tree that survived ("The Tree That Saw Everything") helps to focus meditation, and children have contributed tiles to a mosaic base that surrounds it. The footprint of the destroyed building is outlined by ditches on the ground (this deep trench, a "negative volume", anticipates the dual pools on the site of 9/11 in New York); a faint spurt of water at its centre marks the point of impact of the plane; paths destroyed by the crash are partly highlighted "in alternative materials" and a new walk (which traces the "pathways of the rescuers") crosses the new green space. The different memories of that horrible event and hope for the future are drawn into a quiet and undemonstrative whole.

For the design of the Invalidenpark in Berlin in the 1990s (Figure 5.3) Christophe Girot faced equally tough, if different, historical memories, and his design was promoted by a determination to make this "new Berlin" look to the future and not the past, not least because, as he noted after its completion, "this memory … [will] become fainter with time". The site itself was layered on a parade ground from the 19th century, a wooded parkland designed by Peter Joseph Lenné, a memorial chapel from 1891 to commemorate the Franco-Prussian war that was subsequently destroyed during WWII and that then, during the communist regime, lay buried under the area which the East German police used "as a makeshift staging area for border control, one block from the Berlin Wall and the Invalidenstrasse checkpoint".[11] The memorial's most striking feature − a "Sinking Wall" − may mimic the destroyed Berlin Wall, which now seems to be subsiding into the ground amid a reflecting pool, with water flowing down the granite wedge. The pool itself is based on the footprint of the 19th-century church, and its placement is set askew in the strict geometry of the streetscape, as if to register something at odds with the area, while the whole site itself, tilted at a barely

---

10 *Territories*, pp.76–7, and Udo Weilacher, *In Gardens: Profiles of Contemporary European Landscape Architecture* (Basel, Switzerland: Birkhäuser, 2005), p.43, where there is a detailed account of this "memorial" and the afterlife of the residents there; but people in Amsterdam did not want "a traditional memorial" (*In Gardens*). That sentiment has been echoed elsewhere in Jenny Holzer's "anti-monument" (*In Gardens*, p.55) at Nordhorn on the German/Dutch border, on the site of a much earlier and controversial memorial to those killed in earlier wars; Holzer used another single (apple) tree to mark the centre of a "black garden". She discusses this design in "The Black Garden: Der Garten als Anti-Memorial", *Kunstforum International,* 145 (1999), p.89.

11 This and other information from *Groundswell: Constructing the Contemporary Landscape*, ed. Peter Reed (New York: Museum of Modern Art, 2005), pp.70–3 and *In Gardens,* pp.58 ff. Quotations by Girot are in "Traces into the Future", *Zeitgeist Berlin Invalidenpark* (Zürich: gta Verlag, 2006). I am also grateful to Aislynn Herbst who researched this site for me.

FIGURE 5.3 Invalidenplatz, Berlin, Germany. (Photo: Jennifer Current).

perceptible angle, is acknowledged best at the edges, where a careful, slight threshold leads visitors down into the space. Girot hides the references – the footprint of the former chapel, even the former wall itself: "the narrative", he says, "is hidden in the abstraction of the wedge"; as is the woodland, with some trees from the original space, and ginkgo trees around the water basin ("ancient symbols of hope and perseverance"). Kids play on the wedge, climbing it into the sky.

Battlefield sites are about envisaging the lie of the land, and the armies that manoeuvred over them, but not (usually) about the manipulation of the land-form by modern designers. Much literature, on-site guidance and museums can help us to recover them; but of course what we want to see is the place of encounter "as it was". If we have read about the Battle of Waterloo in Stendhal or Byron, we may respond to its history, but the presentation of the battle today, as set out in W.G. Sebald's narrative of his visit to the actual site, required "a falsification of history".[12] In the Waterloo Panorama, "housed in an immense domed rotunda" ("a circus-like structure"), he could view a painting of the battle "in every direction" ("it is like being at the centre of events"). Across a cluster of life-sized, wax figures of horses, wounded and dying soldiers and hussars, all dressed in "splendid uniforms ... to all appearances authentic", he gazed at a vast (110 × 12 yards) mural, painted in 1915. Yet this "representation" barely touched his memory of the death of "fifty thousand soldiers and ten thousand horses", and neither could he know where they were all buried, for all he sees is "silent brown soil"; neither a recording on the battle in the

---

12 *The Rings of Saturn* (New York: New Directions paperback, 1998), pp.124–6.

Rotunda, given in Flemish, nor the copses of trees planted on the other side of the Channel near Brighton in remembrance of the Battle of Waterloo, help Sebald recover any true vision of what was after all a momentous encounter between the British and the French. It was only when he closed his eyes and saw the action with the hero of Stendhal "wandering the battlefield" that it seemed to come alive in his imagination.

Among American battlefields, Gettysburg[13] is by far the most resonant memorial, as contested as the site of the original battles in 1863 and the conflict between north and south. That Lincoln's famous and brief Address at Gettysburg was delivered on site does fix the place itself in the American consciousness, and the reverberations of that speech, as well as the plethora of memorials and memorial objects, mark it both nationally (ideologically) and locally (geographically), such that it cannot be anywhere else but here. But as regards the availability of some understanding of this "historical ground", Gettysburg is so overwhelmed by accretions of information, books that plot in detail the manoeuvres (hour by hour) during the three-day battle that still seem to be refought in retrospect from different sides, the reworking and reordering or reclamation of the original landscape by the National Park Service – all this plethora of information make the site hard to understand: the conspectus of imagery is overwhelming – statues, inscriptions (including names scratched by soldiers around the battlefield), the commemoration of a host of different militias, infantry and cavalry battalions, individual gravesites and mass cemeteries, markers to commemorate events like that for the "first shot fired", and the buildings and farms used by the two sides during the battle. The overview provided by the 1883 Cyclorama of the battle in the National Military Park Visitor Center is strangely more satisfying than Sebald implied when he saw a similar panorama at Waterloo, yet it, too, invents a landscape that modern eyes need more time and patience to envisage. History here out performs the site, as perhaps it needs must.

Flanders Fields in Belgium was the WWI battleground where so many soldiers lost their lives in the to-and-fro across a wretched, shifting, no-man's land. Their deaths cannot always be individually remembered, since so many were unrecorded or their bodies not recovered; but the site of so much tragedy and bloodshed has called for some memorial, not least because it is still a scar tissue that hurts us. The territory of Flanders Fields itself has been recorded movingly in poems, novels and films that begin to bear witness to that horror for those who fought there. But that landscape still needs to offer comfort to the horrors of this miserable war and, more generally, for those scarred by other 20th-century wars. For people not born before

---

13 I use David Petruzzi, *The Complete Gettysburg Guide: Walking and Driving Tours of the Battlefield, Town, Cemeteries, Field Hospital Sites, and other Topics of Historical Interest* (New York: Savas Beatie, 2009); Mark Grimsley, *Gettysburg: A Battlefield Guide (The Hallowed Ground: Guides to Civil War)* (Lincoln, NB, University of Nebraska Press, 1999); and the Gettysburg website http://www.nps.gov/gett/forteachers/suggestedreading.htm. Also Gary Wills, *Lincoln at Gettysburg: The Words That Remade America* (New York: Simon and Schuster, 1992).

72 History found and exploited in a specific place

1914–18 (increasingly the majority), the duration of that sorrow may not last unless the landscape itself is made to bear witness for lost lives and for those who once lived and farmed there.

So the Portuguese firm PROAP proposed a Remembrance Park along 70 kms of no-man's land – parks dedicated to both Memory and Oblivion (Figure 5.4).[14] So much agricultural land was erased on the battleground, or those battlegrounds were subsequently obliterated by subsequent farming. But in addition this erasure was aided by those who wished to forget its scars, even though 3 million people died there. So PROAP ensured that throughout that same territory that it would honour both memory and oblivion. Yet the battleground was too much in the past for any precise discrimination of where and what action had taken place, so it was a site especially prone to oblivion, even while it was also a place that yearned for an adequate memory of those who died there. More importantly, the site needed to respond to how we thought about the past, including our forgetfulness about it, and to how we might meditate the future, since history is often invoked as a guide for what is to come.

The two "parks" were in fact coterminous: memories would be signalled by remnants of the war and oblivion by evidence of voluntary (or deliberate) erasures of it. The paths would often overlap or intersect, since we recall and forget with equal ease; the paths would converge on sacred places, that were marked both by signs of war and features of the landscape itself. The proposal also wanted visitors to approach the parks through gates, doors or over thresholds, liminal points of awareness about what was about to be experienced (some of which are shown in their preliminary images in Figure 5.4; here figures explore and respond to the landscape).[15] The thrust of such a design would have educated those with no personal memories of the first world war, as it also etched on the landscape signs of its history.

PROAP have made something of a name for themselves in honouring historical sites. Their dialogue between memory and oblivion in Flanders Fields is carried over into other sites as a means of exploring the concept of time, nor were they afraid to invoke contemporary time or culture with its new technologies in both physical and virtual formats. Not obviously literal memorials, their projects can record historical ground with a strong inclination to recall, maybe even with touches of nostalgia for, the lost or fragmented past. "Cities are made of the time of [present-day] gathering and the *time that comes before it*".[16]

---

14 *Concursos Perdidos* [Lost Competitions] (Lisbon; PROAP, 2011), in Portuguese and English; the project for Flanders Fields, pp.26–9.

15 Cf. "How we step through from space to space, the transitions from outward to inward, lies at the core of deep emotion": Lawrence Halprin, "Nature into Landscape into Art", *Landscape in America,* ed. G.F. Thompson (Austin: University of Texas Press, 1995), p.244. The need for and observance of thresholds, both physical and implied, is a key element in much historical ground (see index).

16 *Concursos Perdidos* [Lost Competitions], p. 72, my italics.

History found and exploited in a specific place **73**

FIGURE 5.4 PROAP, four details of the proposed memorial parkland dedicated to Memory and Oblivion in Flanders Fields, Belgium. (Courtesy of the designer).

74 History found and exploited in a specific place

The Garden of Forgiveness (Hadiqat As-Samah) in Beirut shared the same ambition with many other fine memorial projects: to memorialize, in this case, centuries of conflict and warring faiths, and to invite forgiveness for those conflicts after the most recent war in Lebanon had come to an end (Figure 5.5).[17] The site is in the historical centre of Beirut, destroyed during the 16-year civil war, at the conclusion of which archaeology was able to explore the 5.7 acre landscape. Old roads and house foundations were unearthed, including the footprints of different places of worship.

The firm of Kathryn Gustafson and Neil Porter was selected to re-envisage how this space could be created as the first public garden in Beirut and at the same time draw attention to the long history of this ancient cultural landscape from Roman times to the present day. They relied on a variety of strategies: plants were selected to represent the various regions of the country – from its mountains, clearly evidenced in the upper, green section of the site, to the coast, evoked by Judas trees, olive groves, and citrus trees from the Mediterranean. Visitors also enter this sequence (another threshold) by passing over an oblong pool, reminiscent of the *chahar bagh* in Islamic gardens, with two crosswalks; the reminiscence of Islam is there, as is a mosque and Christian churches, yet the historical formulae are not insisted upon nor slavishly represented; yet the plurality of this country's history is clear for all to see. As we proceed down the central *allée* from the *chahar bagh,* there are three religious buildings to our right, with a further three across the bottom of the site, and then we enter the archaeological site, where the designers echoed the typical Roman cross-streets of north–south (*cardo*) and east–west (*decumanus*); among the gardens established in the foundations are herbs used in Roman cooking, medicine and dyeing. Across the lower end of the site is a pergola that protects the bedrock on which these lower religious buildings sit; the signs of mediaeval streets are thrown by shadows of the pergola onto the pavement beneath, and roses ("a flower that originated in the Middle East") are beginning to climb over its structure.

Kathryn Gustsfson and Neil Porter invoke both historical time and geographical reference (since time is made more telling by rooting it in local circumstance). Given the culture of Lebanon and the evident remains that lie in and around the Hadiqat As-Samah, it would be hard for visitors to miss how much they tread on historical ground and recognize the different faiths that have peopled the city; yet the design is also "layered" mentally, as visitors presumably come to learn the different plants and the signposts of earlier cultures, and recognize the residual layout of roads and street systems. In fact, the palimpsestial nature of the design was based upon an old child's map of Lebanon, which the designers annotated/overlaid with phrases ("ancient relics", geological forms, "the tradition of garden making",

---

17 The design is set out briefly in *Groundswell*; quotations from this are used in my text. Other considerations of this site are taken up by Raffaella Fabiani Giannetto in the nostalgia issue of *Change Over Time* (Spring, 2013) and in Neil Porter, "Past, Present, and Future: Designing areas across many lands and cultures", *Topos*, 80 (2012), pp.61–5.

History found and exploited in a specific place 75

FIGURE 5.5 Kathryn Gustafson and Neil Porter, plan for the Garden of Forgiveness. (Hadiqat As-Samah), Beirut (courtesy of the designers).

76 History found and exploited in a specific place

etc.) that controlled how they eventually came to see that forgiveness and prosperity could remake Beirut ("metaphors for unity"). It is a powerful affirmation for the design to fulfil: one can only hope that Beirut learns from the contemporary work as the designers did from the past.

A memorial of a different sort was established in Manchester, UK; different, in that there is no visual or even verbal suggestion of what triggered the event – an IRA bomb that tore apart the city in 1996 – and little chance that Mancunians will remember it in fifty years' time, not least because there is no record of it on site. The name of Exchange Square could have many meanings, but the one that clearly does resonate is the desire to draw together – to exchange – the old and the new city in the wake of the explosion,[18] and to do so by re-inventing or recovering a mediaeval ditch between the two segments of the site.

On one side of the Square are the older buildings, including the historic Corn Exchange, and the precincts of the Cathedral; on the other, a brand new Marks and Spencer store. Between the two, the ground (Figure 5.6) is marked in front of the new store by a striped, austere pavement with seats in the form of trolleys

FIGURE 5.6 Exchange Square, Manchester, UK. (Courtesy of Martha Schwartz).

18 See Martha Schwartz, *Recycling Spaces, Curating Urban Evolution: The work of Martha Schwartz Partners* (Novato, CA: ORO Editions, 2011), pp.44–67. Quotations are from this text. Also *The Vanguard Landscapes and Gardens of Martha Schwartz*, ed. Tim Richardson (London: Thames & Hudson, 2004), pp.72–7. Several of her proposals for Exchange Square were not acted upon (the moveable trolleys, for example) and since the Square was established in 2000 the city has been cluttered the site with irrelevant items like a Ferris wheel.

History found and exploited in a specific place **77**

(a memory of Manchester's railway era, originally designed to be movable), and by six curved rows of seating of warm yellow puddingstone that face, amphitheatre-like, the older facades of the city. These are places where people "hang out' and see the city sights (as both audience and performers), and the one event that draws their attention is the line of the mediaeval (so-called) Hanging Ditch.

This once marked an edge of the early town, and Martha Schwartz has resurrected the ditch as a curved riverbed, filled with large and irregular stepping stones on which the children love to play. Three pipes pull water from below and gush it into the ditch until it disappears at the further end of its arc. The re-assertion of that mediaeval ditch, transposed into a modern fountain and play area, yet slyly inserting the idea that its form is not "quite" modern, is a historical marker that need not deflect those who love to use it, whether or not they know its mediaeval origin. A further proposal for the Manchester site, unrealized, was far less histor-ically motivated: rows of metallic palm trees on the upper level were, apparently, to mimic or recall the "cast-iron column with painted copper palm leaves in the Great Kitchen of Brighton's Royal Pavilion, designed by John Nash in the early nineteenth century". Fun as that might be, and reminiscent of other fake palm trees by Schwartz,[19] they ceased (as far as I can see) to have any reason for being in Manchester, other than perhaps a vague gesture towards its industrial past. Exchange Square has effectively ceased to be a memorial site, and takes us therefore into designs where a recollection of the past is largely invented.

Another issue (postponed for the moment) is how long any memory of a historical ground will last, absent some intervention by designers to highlight its memorial feature or some posted account of its original disaster. Designers like Schwartz can highlight, in their own writings and others' commentaries, how the occasion of the site has been understood, but there is little encouragement to sustain those memories once it has been built. We may all have "memories" of the Battles of Waterloo or Gettysburg, as they are not only etched in the national consciousness or mythology, but their sites are preserved and memorialized as battlefields; but what of places with a strong or local, but in the end limited, memorial hold on those that go there?

There are other "monuments" to the past that also address something in the future rather than simply memorialize a past event. Robert Smithson's "A Tour of the Monuments of Passaic, New Jersey" from 1967 pays a deliberately un-sensational visit to the Passaic River, armed with his instamatic camera ("what rationalists call a camera").[20] Through this viewfinder he observes a series of industrial sites, an ironic yet celebratory picturesque: a giant pipe, a cluster of six

19 See her design for work for the Broward County Civic Arena, Florida, with sixteen canopies of steel and coloured vinyl that recall displaced trees from the Everglades: *Vanguard Landscapes*, p.107.

20 *The Collected Writings*, ed. Jack Flam (Berkeley, CA: University of California Press, 1996), pp.68–74; see also Jennifer L. Roberts, *Mirror-Travels: Robert Smithson and History* (New Haven, CT: Yale University Press, 2004), where this particular essay by Smithson is positioned within an elaborate survey of Smithson's perspectives on history (pp.62–85).

78 History found and exploited in a specific place

gushing pipes (he terms them "fountains"), a crater, a sand box, concrete abutments for a new bridge, used car lots, and so on. He refuses, happily, any "crass" anthropomorphizing – the great pipe that psychoanalysts might see as some huge sexual organ – Smithson merely says that it was "there". The place is "confounded into a unitary chaos", without a rational past and without any sign of "the 'big' events of history". Jennifer Roberts sees these as "lethargic" monuments, drawing upon the word that derives from the Greek *Lethe*, the mythical river in Hades whose waters cause drinkers to forget their past". But in fact, as she argues, Smithson converts the historical past of Passaic into an "impending future"; it possesses "no past – just what passes for a future". Passaic is still replete with what he still hails as "monuments", though not what "universities" would "foster" as worthy of study. Taking up one of his favourite themes, entropy, what he sees in Passaic are only the makings of ruins in reverse: today's ruins that would *become* buildings.

His "monuments" are a strange and intriguing paean to a future or futurist life for sites that are dysfunctional. His "snapshots", says Roberts, "preclude memory, even as they preserve it". But unlike what landscape architects and builders would do by re-envisaging or re-formatting a new life for post-industrial detritus, and though he may celebrate "what passes for a future" that is yet to be, he rests his case on what "rationalist" photography shows him was "there". While Smithson's Passaic might be read as anticipating recent moves to address the dross or drosscapes of derelict sites, his stance may be seen to parody what landscape architects have or might take up.

Drosscapes and others

One of the largest issues to confront contemporary landscape architects is how to respond to a host of urban and industrial decay: dying city centres, industries that die or are depleted, the huge and often dismaying remains of power plants, steel mills, gas works, waste-water treatment plants, sewage plants, and coal mines. These confrontations have elicited several landscape responses, like Martha Schwartz's book on *Recycling Urban Spaces* and its extended title, *Curating Urban Evolution*, along with a great variety of interventions chronicled in issues of *Lotus* and *Topos* magazines and in many European designs for these abandoned sites.[21] Yet, as we saw in Chapter Four with the disbanded factory for Citroën or the former Dépôt des Vins in Paris, this often has taken the form of dismantling the former site and buildings upon it without much, or even any, allusion to what was originally there. This is perhaps changing. Schwartz's title and her book ask for landscape architects to "curate" the urban mess. One element of that curatorial response is to deploy historical resonances.

21 See *Topos* issue on "Culturescapes", 78 (2012), pp.28–35 for the rediscovery of Manchester's "Lost River" and a discussion of sewage treatment plant in Bottrop, Germany (pp.56–60) and an old coal mine at Zollverein, designed by Agence T, a listed World Heritage Site. See also the volumes *Fieldwork* and *On Site*.

Remains of former, usually industrial buildings have produced some remarkable instances of how derelict sites may present some historical event while also curating the adjacent land. One of the earliest (famous) examples of a gas works saved and used as a structure was created by Richard Haag in Seattle, WA. He envisaged how the rusting structures could be a feature of, and in, a new parkland; it would be an industrial folly for a modern age, with little interest in recreating similar oddities that the European picturesque garden boasted in its prime[22]; the former gas works could elicit its own, modern fantasies. But now, fenced off and inaccessible to users of the park, and with continuing toxic emissions from the landfill, the structure somewhat loses its power. Maybe its removal and more remediation of the soil, while keeping the name of Gas Works Park, would actually trigger some interest in the origin of the name.

The term "drosscape", meaning derelict, toxic or waste land, was used by Alan Berger as a title for his book, *Drosscape: Wasting Land in Urban America* in 2006, his title coined from a remark by the Elizabethan poet, Edmund Spenser in 1585, that "All world's glory is but dross unclean". The reference also contains the implication that dross is "wasted" gold that can still be cleaned and re-used (so the new alchemists are to be urban designers). The dirty, unclean world of sprawl, downtowns, commercial corridors, landfills, railroad facilities, electrical lines, spaghetti highway interchanges, shipping terminals and abandoned infrastructure does not immediately seem part of a lost world the history of which merits recovery, and there is little room in Berger's often forensic analysis to ask how the history of these sites might be, or could be, recuperated and the world's "glory" restored (at least in this book – another is promised on that topic). His photographs are fascinating and advance a convincing sense of how "drosscape may be visually pleasing", at least for his shrewd and attentive camera ("a Contax 645 with Fuji Velvia film"[23]). He asks the landscaper – and he himself was trained as one – to move beyond "design" and to collaborate and negotiate with those who could produce the "integration of waste landscape in the urban world". But designers have already, and not just in the United States, worked to integrate drosscapes into a functional, urban world, and in so doing they revive a strong sense of the past, its decay and its future for new users.

With the large-scale disappearance of many shipping and industrial areas along inland rivers, designers have found a rich opportunity for new types of parkland. In Philadelphia, the Delaware River, once a busy destination for commercial shipping and pleasure cruises, now has a series of derelict piers jutting into the river, with little scope for linking the water with the city behind (not helped, it is true, by the expressway that cuts the city off even more from the water) and with

---

22 See John Dixon Hunt, *The Picturesque Garden in Europe* (Thames & Hudson, New York, 2002 and London, 2003). German edition, *Der malerische Garten* (Stuttgart: Verlag Eugen Ulmer, 2004).

23 Alan Berger, *Drosscape: Wasting Land in Urban America* (New York: Princeton Architectural Press, 2006), pp.12–13 and 15.

little incentive to tempt people down along its banks.[24] A master plan is designed to rehabilitate four segments of the waterfront, in one of which a new park has been created. Municipal Pier 11, the Race Street Pier, was refashioned by Field Operations who won the competition to start the re-enhancement of the river and to create a series of green spaces or urban parklets along the Delaware.

What had risen originally on the pier in the early years of the 20th century was a handsome Municipal pavilion, with observation towers over the water and decorated with cornices and pilasters on the city facade. Its upper floor, or Pleasure Pavilion, housed a variety of public functions, while the lower level dealt with local shipping. Essentially geared for a working class who could not reach the more fancy resorts of either Coney Island or the nearer Atlantic City, this pier allowed them some chance of realizing both the fun of active and passive seaside (at least along the waterside).[25] What Field Operations did was to divide the pier, not vertically as in the original building, but horizontally along its length, with two connected levels (Figure 5.7): a more active, upper one, slightly tilted so that you look upwards over the river as you walk its length, and the lower one, much closer to the water for more passive reaction, and marked with slivers of lawn and trees.

FIGURE 5.7 Philadelphia, Municipal Pier II, designed by Field Operations. (Photo: Emily T. Cooperman).

24 This disruption will, in fact, now be "curated" by a new proposal by George Hargreaves Associates for re designing Penn's Landing at Philadelphia: http://planphilly.com/articles/2013/04/04/drwc-names-hargreaves-to-design-penn-s-landing-re-do.
25 I am indebted here to an essay by my student Purva Chawla and her citation of a 1992 University of Pennsylvania Historical Preservation thesis on these Municipal piers.

They merge at the water's edge, where people are closest to and can observe the river, down stairs between the levels. Railings recall handrails on ocean liners, and the wood-plastic composite material mimics seaside boardwalks. The historical gesture is modest, but, Genette-like, alludes to other "texts"; it conveys in unmistakably modern ways a sense of what was originally here on Pier 11.

Michael Van Valkenburgh's Brooklyn Bridge Park, immediately to the south of the bridge itself, takes on a cluster of derelict piers immediately below the Brooklyn–Queens Expressway (Figure 5.8).[26] These are to be turned into a series of different parks – alas, the opportunity to move between them across a pedestrian bridge ("wave-attenuating boardwalks") was scuppered by the city, so that visitors must return to the mainland before exploring another park; some of these will be wetlands and salt marshes, others recreational fields and sport courts, lawns and beaches, boating areas and marinas, café and picnic areas, viewing platforms; behind the piers and along the inner edges of the river are buildings for development, including a former tobacco warehouse. The site is designed to provide a framework for the various activities and ecologies, not least the "views, smells and sounds of the water's edge". The ground and its watery edges (many different forms of this are envisaged) are certainly and variously historical, acknowledging New Yorkers' legendary appetite for the water. A local determined community voiced clearly over the last twenty years how much they wanted access to the water; but the design also ensures that there is no obscuring of Brooklyn Heights behind the site (also demanded by the community), as well as a future need to find new

FIGURE 5.8 Brooklyn Bridge Park, New York City. (Photo: Gideon Fink Shapiro).

26 Ethan Carr, "Brooklyn Bridge Park: The Complex Edge", in *Reconstructing Urban Landscapes*, pp.235–53, with preliminary computer projections of the proposed park. Quotations are from this essay.

82 History found and exploited in a specific place

associations for the lost commercial life that once absorbed the edges of the city. While designers and critics may readily recall, as does Ethan Carr, Herman Melville's "crowds of water-gazers" or similar enthusiasms from Walt Whitman and others, these memories will not sustain the new park, any more than they did when commercial infrastructure in the 19th century blocked people from the river. Now it will be the folk who relish new ecological opportunities, not just the views, and who experience the transformed and physical connections with the river, that will make Brooklyn Bridge Park a new historical ground.

Similar refurbishments and new visions have become a contemporary parkland experience, alongside rivers, but also in the toxic and industrial acreage of places, like Duisburg-Nord Landscape Park by Peter Latz + Partner. This park is extremely well-known, the most famous of all industrial "reclamations" or "reinventions", which landscape architects worldwide acclaim.[27] The colossal remains dwarf its users, and the designer did not want in his turn to erect anything that would begin to challenge the enormity of this derelict steel plant. Its success, apart from the crowds that throng it, is that it acknowledges and celebrates the original site, granting fresh opportunities for the use of its remains: lofty walls allow people to practice climbing, scuba diving is available in large tanks, raised industrial walkways are reformulated to allow visitors to observe the remains from on-high, gardens fill spaces of former sintering bunkers and retention pools and are filled with pioneer plants that will flourish is this toxic soil (Figure 5.9), huge steel plates form an amphitheatre for plays and concerts, and, to the observant eye, old machinery (buckets that once poured molten steel, chimney fragments) serve as "garden" imagery of fountains and sculpture. Indeed, identifying and re-presenting such rusted items allow a wholly fresh perspective on industrial remains.[28]

Not every design can so accommodate and declaim its historical ground as does Duisburg. Simply by leaving so much on site – towering blast furnaces and other infrastructure – that no visitor can avoid, yet augmenting it with subtle and incidental new uses and plantings, Duisburg not only establishes a formidable example of historical ground in a part of Germany once renowned for its heavy industry, but draws attention to its present and indeed future fame. The Ruhr region that transformed a once agricultural landscape into a powerful coal and steel industry was, by the late 1980s, one of the most devastated regions in Europe. That the structures at Duisburg will ultimately need maintenance and conservation themselves should not diminish its historical importance in a 21st-century Germany.

27 The "curating" designs of Peter Latz + Partner are discussed in Udo Weilacher, *Syntax of Landscape: The Landscape Architecture of Peter Latz and Partners* (Basel: Birkhäuser, 2008), particularly the section "Dealing with 'bad places'", pp.79–166. See also Weilacher's collection of short essays by various authors on this site to honour Peter Latz's 80th birthday, *Learning from Duisburg Nord* (Munich, Germany: Technische Universität, 2009).
28 The photographer Alyssha Eve Csük, a resident of Bethlehem, PA, with its steelworks that finally closed in 1995, has produced some beautiful images of corrosion, and the weeping puddles, vivid with iron oxide, in her "Abstract Portraits of Steel". See *New York Times,* 15 May, 2011.

History found and exploited in a specific place **83**

FIGURE 5.9 Peter Latz + Partner, gardens in the Duisburg-Nord Landscape Park, Germany.

The Ruhr has attracted a variety of proposals beyond that of Duisburg Nord to emend, clarify, or entertain its new inhabitants and users. Topographical play with the forms of farmed land was proposed by Paolo Bürgi (see Chapter 2) and endorsed by a farmer who was happy to see his fields both used and appreciated by those not involved in their agriculture. Martha Schwartz, too, has re-energized an historical agricultural landscape. Both Bürgi and Schwartz rely, respectively, upon the International Building Exhibition Berlin (Internationale Bauausstellung

84 History found and exploited in a specific place

Berlin; IBA Berlin), that looks to restore the Emscher Park, and a municipal and local consortium; both worked with the local farmers.[29]

Schwartz took up an invitation to provide a temporary installation in fields outside the former coal city of Gelsenkirchen, where she was required to build "sustainably" and to pay for the project by crops harvested there. Overlooked by a statue of the "Iron" Chancellor, Otto von Bismarck, on an adjacent hilltop, the fields below were planted, reaped and the hay baled in black plastic bags that were then formed into a small circular, 2-metre high room; below the bales a coal floor reminded visitors of past industry. More bales, now in red plastic (supposedly the colour of power, since electric lines crossed the field overhead, to signal both industrial power and the power of Bismarck in unifying Germany) formed a narrow pathway up the hill towards the Iron Chancellor; from his hilltop, visitors could see the agricultural landscape anew. They looked down on a field planted with corn that paralleled the power lines, interspersed at right angles with bare earthen strips between rectangles of clover; straight rows of corn also branched out strangely alongside the clover and earth, fanning out into the shape of a "baroque" garden. At summer's end, the field would be ploughed under and re-sown.

Peter Latz himself has also undertaken projects at Saarbrücken Harbour Island, and at the Parco Dora in Turin[30] that also abuts a curve of its river, to make new parks without denying the essential rudiments of the older industry: the plan for the former weaves together a variety of historical items – a garden theatre, manicured hedges, a regular grove of trees, axial pathways that recall the rail lines on which the harbour cranes originally moved, all of which enter into an intricate dialogue with what remains of the industrial site, the walls of rubble, the leavings of much debris, gradually being covered over with plants, the huge bridge of the 1980s autobahn that cuts through the middle of the park and over the river, and a brand new "ruin" or water gate that stands in a pool below that roadway. Latz draws his inspiration from the old (the Mausoleum of Augustus in Rome) and the new (the Parque del Clot in Barcelona, though it too recalls older forms). He delights in what can remain, but makes no attempt to indulge in false historicity, with no reference to the destruction of the harbour in WWII or any attempt to restore the arm of the River Saar that was filled in during the 1960s.

In Turin, too, surviving structures of industrial buildings were saved from demolition – 30 steel columns that supported the huge roof (now demolished) of the Vitali steel mill stand like massive columns along a processional way; down their length will be raised walkways, as at Duisburg, with flower beds beneath and plants growing over other concrete lumps (Figure 5.10). The cooling tower of the

---

29 *Recycling Spaces*, pp.137–49 and *The Vanguard Landscapes*, pp.144–7. Two slightly different takes by Latz and Schwartz on this agricultural ground. Latz's site is also touched upon in the book cited in the next footnote.

30 See Udo Weilacher, *Syntax of Landscape*, pp.82 ff and 134 ff. Also Latz + Partners design for the riverside walkway at Kranzberg.

FIGURE 5.10 Peter Latz + Partner, steel columns in the Parc Dora, Turin, Italy. (Courtesy of Latz + Partner).

Michelin factory further on the site also remains, and is illuminated at night. These strong industrial signatures make a very different claim for historical ground from either Duisburg or Saarbrücken: the latter is complex, the former overwhelming with the physical weight of the massive infrastructures and sly insertion of community life, whereas the more open spaces of the Turin park are dedicated far more to life in a densely built-up area of the city, with clear connections to the residential area and its shopping. Yet Latz also noted that it takes "70 to 80 years of time and care" before a park can fully develop its new potential and absorb the vestiges of its industrial past.[31]

Attention to climate change and its impact on river edges, along with the challenge to respond to post-industrial sites on both the Greenwich Peninsular in England and the Garonne riverfront in France,[32] impelled Michel Desvigne to invoke different geomorphic features for his "intermediate landscape" (an odd phrase really), a "kind of Ur-landscape" that "might" have existed there historically in earlier times. In France this involves the invention of a new landscape, natural river banks, marshlands, meadows and woodland, not found in the barren

---

31 Ibid, p. 141.
32 *Groundswell*, pp.152–5 (for the Garonne Riverfront Master Plan) and pp.148–51 (for the Greenwich Peninsula). See also *Intermediate Natures: The Landscapes of Michel Desvigne* (Basel: Birkhäuser, 2009), and *Lotus,* 150 (2012), pp.12–15.

86 History found and exploited in a specific place

conditions of an industrial landscape, but one that we might presume to have "existed centuries before", in other words an invented or "feigned" parkland; hence one that is "intermediate" between an imagined past and a projected future. On the English site, where again no "existing landscape" existed – it had been the site of a huge gasworks and more recently of the Millennium Dome by the Richard Rogers partnership – Desvigne envisaged an alluvial forest, that might have existed on the peninsula, and he drew upon forest plantations elsewhere in Oxfordshire to establish a woodland of hornbeam and shrubs, which could later be thinned out to introduce birch, alder and oak, a system that draws attention to the "temporal dimension" of the scheme. Perhaps this is, in fact, more of an "invented landscape", and with others is best taken up in the next chapter.

Another impressive and far more conspicuous intervention from the architects De Miguel, Munoz & Correl was the Parque de Cabecera in Valencia, Spain. Along the former bed of the river Turia, where 18th-century dykes protected the town from flooding, their design borrowed the idea of small islets in the river for a sequence of different zones: hillocks covered with trees drop into the water, another hillock marks where the river takes a 90-degree turn, wooden pontoons and walkways conduct visitors along the water, and local rocks form generous curves across the landscape, paralleling and mimicking the bends of the river.[33] So too the firm Atelier Bruel-Delmar adapts the riverbanks along the Meurthe River in Nancy to engage with the city behind them, lining the sides of the river with gabion walls and with slopes to accommodate rising water, yet allowing pedestrian access to the quays and using the dam as a link between the left and right banks.[34]

Remembrance of things past

The remembrance of the past is a leitmotif of many famous novels and films: Evelyn Waugh's *Brideshead Revisited*, Anthony Powell's *A Dance to the Music of Time*, or Marcel Proust's *A la recherche du temps perdu*. And as it touches upon nostalgia (think Downton Abbey), it seems to be not only a modern but an increasingly contemporary fixation.[35] But remembering past time for landscape architects is not exactly as it was with Marcel Proust and his madeleine. What triggers an individual does not translate readily to how a landscape can recall events or earlier formulations on the site for many visitors. Associations, floating and weaving in the

---

33 *l'architecture d'aujourd'hui*, 363 (March/April, 2006), pp.94–9. Other riverfronts and fluvial designs are discussed under the condition of weather in Chapter Two. A recent group of waterfronts is discussed also in *Lotus*, 150 (2012), pp.8–11 (the waterfront at Almere in the Netherlands by Desvigne), the proposed Qianhai Waterfront City by Field Operations (pp.60–3), and the WEST 8 one at Madrid Rio (pp.66–73).

34 *Territories*, pp.22–3.

35 This obsession is exhaustively, even forensically, discussed by David Lowenthal in both his early book *The Past is a Foreign Country* and in his essay in the "Nostalgia" issue of the preservation journal, *Change Over Time: An international journal of conservation and the built environment* (Spring, 2013).

mind, can sustain a world of recollections, but will not easily, if at all, sustain a physical design. Nor is it easy to rely upon a designer's sense of what a madeleine would do for him or her, since a madeleine, so to speak, tastes differently for everyone, and some people may not even know what it is. And there is also the pull of nostalgia, not to be denied perhaps, but less likely to enable a design that, again, must address a wider community.

One striking example of this lack of associative recognition in an older landscape, that I find particularly intriguing, is William Kent's Praeneste Terrace at Rousham, in Oxfordshire. Clearly derived from Kent's knowledge of the antique Temple of Fortune at Palestrina (i.e. Praeneste in Roman times) and drawing on his nostalgia for Italy where he spent nine years, this takes just one single arcade of the ancient Roman complex and situates it on a slope overlooking the local River Cherwell. The name of the terrace was obviously known and its provenance understood in the family for whom Kent reworked the existing garden, and for Kent it must have been a veritable "madeleine" to remind him of his years as a designer in Italy. But apparently the name was not known to the steward when he wrote to remind the absent family how wonderful the place was and listed its many features.[36] So the arcade did not prompt the steward with any association, nor does it resonate with any but garden historians who study Rousham.

Some well devised triggers can work well for a wider audience. In Chapter Two Adriaan Geuze was quoted on the lost opportunities of an older Dutch landscape, squandered by development and bureaucracy. One of his more nostalgic designs from 2003 addressed a lingering nostalgia for this landscape of fields, waterways, windmills and farmed land. His "Horizon Project" (Figure 5.11) places three 8-metre high cows along a road, with an old windmill in the distance, "as a reminder of the unique Dutch horizon" in this heavily built-up coastal zone (the Randstad) from Rotterdam to Amsterdam.[37] Slyly referencing a Paul Potter painting, *The Bull*, from c.1647 (it hangs in the Mauritshuis), where a wide Netherlandish landscape to the far horizon is glimpsed through the bull's legs, Geuze's tethered and inflatable cows gaze benignly at the passing traffic; neighbouring farmers gladly offered land for this satire that reveres as well as pillories the erasure of traditional Dutch landscape history. This is undoubtedly nostalgia, but it is both ironic (depending, too, perhaps, on those who know Potter's painting) and, perhaps more importantly, makes passers-by reflect readily on what has been lost along these rural Dutch roads. It is also fun, not a very familiar instinct among landscape architects.

In urban sites, especially those canvassed earlier in this chapter along riverbanks and derelict shipping lanes, even if nostalgia is teasingly presented, it is not enough. Remembrance of the past means certainly knowing what was there and then

36 See John MacClary, "A Description of Rousham", transcribed and edited by Mavis Batey in "The way to view Rousham by Kent's gardener", *Garden History*, 11 (1983), specifically p.130.
37 *Mosaics*, pp.24–7. See also the essay on "The Discovery of the Netherlands" by Olof Koekebakker in *Memory and Transformation* (Rotterdam: NAI Publishers, 2008), pp.33–9.

FIGURE 5.11 Adriaan Geuze, "Horizon Project", with huge inflatable cows in a redolent Dutch landscape. (Courtesy of WEST 8 Urban Design & Landscape Architecture; photo: Jeroen Musch).

recovering memories which, however, are able to sustain new visions, not just fond nostalgia. Two such designs seem to achieve that renewal within the realm of nostalgia: Lassus' Garden of Returns at Rochefort sur Mer and STOSS's Green Bay urban/riverside landscape in Wisconsin.

A signature and now famous landscape design for a moribund waterfront was executed by Bernard Lassus for Rochefort sur Mer (Figure 5.12). His attention to the port's history and his determination to make a new park for the town did not, however, mean a clichéd French parterre, as if a garden were sited around some manorial building. Indeed, the handsome 17th-century building of the Corderie Royale, which was a rope factory – its extravagant length allowed the production of ropes for the French navy, is now used for a variety of other community purposes; in no way could this industrial building be re-thought into being a "chateau". Then there was also Lassus's strong conviction that the town should contrive an economic future out of a once potent botanical past.[38]

The River Charente at Rochefort had been the lifeblood and the *raison d'être* of the town, but it came to be too far from the Atlantic and by the 20th century had silted up. It had once been the port of entry into France of a range of North American plants, brought home by royal command in warships returning from the Americas. Among these specimens was the magnolia, imported from Canada by the Marquis de la Galissonière, and the begonia, named after the town *intendant*, Michel Bégon. This offered a botanical arsenal, as Lassus saw it, to match the lost naval arsenal there that is now dominated only by Louis XIV's huge Corderie Royale, where ropes were no longer fabricated. Lassus however saw that the begonia, by now a plant produced generically throughout Europe and having lost touch with its home "base" at Rochefort, might furnish a role for the revival of the town's

---

38 This site is well known, but bears a fresh scrutiny in the light of ideas for historical grounds. See *The Landscape Architecture of Bernard Lassus*, pp.131–40.

FIGURE 5.12 Bernard Lassus, Le Jardin des Retours, Rochefort sur Mer, France, with the Corderie Royale in the background, and the ramp into the garden from the upper civic parkland marked by lines of Virginia Liriodendron.

botanical past. This it has now, somewhat astonishingly, achieved. The town purchased a begonia collection and now has a breeding station here, and established fairs or "Begionales". So the town, if not the port, has also achieved a return of economic prosperity.

This "Garden of Returns", then, honours that botanical revival, its name recalling the port to which plants "returned" as well as the return of the begonia to a modern pre-eminence. But the town has also had a new park returned to it, a greatly welcomed amenity. There are other physical transformations of this park that mark a similar botanical legacy – a ramp of Virginian *Liriodendron* that leads from an upper municipal park into this one, and a cluster of *Chamaerops* palm trees beside the Corderie. But the remainder of the park has other reminiscences – a restored WWII German dry dock with a full-size display of masts, ropes and rigging, and of baskets (imitated now in concrete) in which plants were returned to France in the 17th and 18th centuries; there is also a labyrinth of naval battles with computer games stationed in its enclosures where we can negotiate fights of the French navy. Down a system of *percées* or cuts through the shrubs and trees on the river bank, we catch glimpses of the once industrial river, where dinghies of a sailing club tack about and their pupils glimpse the former Cordonerie up the same *percées*.

Chris Reed (STOSS Landscape Urbanism) is establishing on both sides of the Fox River in Green Bay, Wisconsin, a new character that gives back to the neighbourhood both a sense of its historical past and a future for the city. At Green Bay, buildings had largely turned their back on the river by the end of the 20th century, or were empty, with redundant spaces used for parking: the city that lay behind saw little interest in the river, had with no relationship with the water or paid little attention to its significance. The river, nonetheless, has been the lifeline of this community since the 17th century, for much longer than the silted-up River Charente at Rochefort, or the River Avon at Bristol in the west of England, both unavailable to large, modern vessels. Here at Green Bay, freighters still ply the river and head out into Lake Michigan, and the sight of them and of the infrastructure that serves them – cranes and derricks, and the raised bridges that allow them to pass down river – are an essential part of the place, past and present. But it is not just that STOSS had made the river approachable, with walkways alongside it (not cantilevered high above the water but accessible to those who stroll there) and where people can sit and watch the river traffic or even hang their legs over the edges of the overlooks. Now small boats can use the river, there will be floats on the water and small space-ship-like crafts to ply there. The river also dialogues now with the city, as urban features are inserted into Citydock (as it is called; Figure 5.13) – condominiums, amphitheatres, offices and retail outlets, then the social activities – cafés, concerts, or children playing in the squirting fountains. And despite the fairly narrow width of the riverside strip (50–60 feet wide), the sense of interpenetration is further enhanced by the streets that emerge onto it or lead back into the city; moreover the "strip" is not straight-edged at the water's edge, but pushes out with

FIGURE 5.13 The riverside walks at Green Bay, Wisconsin. (Photo courtesy of STOSS).

landing stages, docks for small craft, small inlets and overlooks. Its wooden boards, along with the series of seats and benches, recall the timber trade of Green Bay's historical past, though their steel underpinning and brackets are visible and obviously modern. And so are the new wetlands and storm-processing terraces on the far side of the river, for if a historical gesture cannot also provoke a new and modern future it is likely to be merely nostalgic.[39]

By the end of the 20th century many European nations had lost most or all of their colonies, which is, for the former territories, a matter to celebrate; but their loss still resonates at home and may call for some recognition of vanished territories. Another Portuguese firm responded to the loss of historical colonies with their five "Unseen Gardens", "unseen" because they are far away (Brazil, Goa, Macau, etc.) and now just a historical memory. For the 1998 EXPO along the banks of river in Lisbon, João Gomes da Silva drew upon five original Portuguese colonies, recalling their distinctive constructions, planting and pathways, by which modern Portuguese and their visitors could remember a lost empire (Figure 5.14).

FIGURE 5.14 João Gomes da Silva, "Unseen Gardens", Lisbon, Portugal. (Courtesy of the designer).

39 Part of this section on Green Bay is drawn from my remarks written for *Stoss Landscape Urbanism*, in the series of "Source Books in Landscape Architecture" (Columbus, OH: Knowlton School of Architecture, Ohio State University, 2013).

92 History found and exploited in a specific place

Among the losses of the modern world perhaps none is more visible and – for those who suffered cuts in their local networks – more annoying than derelict railway lines; Great Britain was particularly affected by the Beeching cuts of the 1960s. In Chapter Three, a new park in Paris recollected the loss of extensive marshalling yards by stretching the new park along the lines of the former tracks, and thereby enhanced a neighbourhood dearly in need of some such parkland. A much earlier response in Paris to the loss of local rail traffic was the Promenade Plantée, a long elevated track that ran northwards for several kilometres from the vicinity of the Gare de Lyon. Along its length we are always aware that it was a former railroad, poised high above the neighbouring streets, to which from time to time stairs descend. It cuts between apartment blocks, and even opens out into an area that marked a former train stop, though now this grass arena recalls the site of an early chateau of Reuilly. Yet equally along much of the stretch near the Gare de Lyon the elevated tracks are now decorated with trellis works, flower beds (hence the name of the *planted* promenade), and pools around which the paths divide that sometimes make one forget, as the joggers troop by, that we are on top of a former railway line.

That French example spurred, though the acknowledgement was only fitfully made, New York's High Line, an extraordinary (if for neighbours too successful) design. If the Promenade Plantée is useful for joggers, who have sufficient room and a lengthy *trajet,* the High Line is often extremely crowded and fairly short, less a stroll than a spectacle, with seats to watch promenaders, even a glass viewing platform from which to observe people moving on the streets below. Its gesture to the railway is far less firm than that in Paris: but it does pass between buildings, it does occasionally allow glimpses of the street below, and it does occasionally dramatize both the remnants of railway ties and sections of rails with some allusions to what might grow there. Yet the planting is by no means what habitually grows on derelict sidings: the plants were designed by the wonderful Dutch plantsman, Piet Oudolf – elegant grasses flourish between concrete pavers that mimic railway tracks laid lengthwise along the walk (with notices to tell one to "keep off the grass") or contained in cortex steel planters along the sides of the paths. One suspects that any original recall of this former track that brought commercial traffic into the meat district of downtown Manhattan will slowly lose its historical appeal, if it has not already done so.

For some of these sites there is an element of nostalgia, nonetheless, in that it simply recalls the past. One may harbour a personal nostalgia, but public nostalgia needs to be sustained by a more substantial sense of some collective history; and one element of that has probably to be a sense that the past, not merely remembered with fear or happiness, also promises a future that augurs a new existence for a landscape and its use. The Unseen Gardens in Lisbon could be a nostalgic recall of that nation's colonial past and territories overseas, but as its population grows older it is likely to be for many just a new, if unusual park. Many new installations do promise more of what is to come – new uses, new activities, new economic benefits – than just a recall or renewal of any previous existence.

History found and exploited in a specific place 93

Green Bay, Rochefort, High Lines anywhere (and the New York one has become something to be imitated everywhere) – all are places to visit, to see and be seen, but not to dwell on the past. Railroad buffs may dwell with delight on derelict rail lines and lament the loss of a transportation network, and French historians could wax eloquently on the naval prestige of Louis XIV or even of his dedication to plant importation, but those nostalgias there will surrender to their current usefulness as public parks.

The Landscape Architecture Europe Foundation organizes an astonishing and invigorating series of juries to assess and reward new work across Europe, partly to promote the profession and give it identity, partly to showcase that work to people outside Europe. In two volumes, *Fieldwork* (2006) *and On Site* (2009), they feature a wide range of work, some of which inevitably addresses sites coloured by a historical sensibility and a sense, even, of nostalgia. It is, in fact, one of the main themes addressed by competitors and sometimes praised by jurors that such and such a site privileges history. Yet for many designers (and therefore for juries) it is an instinct or a vision for making new work rather than activating some recourse to history, and so inevitably this is also far less evident in the minds of the users or how these finished sites are to be viewed.

For Eduardo Arroyo's design from 1998–99 of a plaza in Barakaldo, in the Basque country, to be situated within an apartment complex, the "core idea" was to recall history, or rather to display the recovered remains of materials around the site, once farmed, then used for shipping and lastly for the making of steel.[40] A grid of abstract rectangles – wood, sand, asphalt, steel – interspersed with squares of water or planting and with right-angled benches at various intervals, the rectangles sometimes rearing up into skateboard slopes, is fun; but it seems a stretch to see this collage of found materials throughout the patterned plaza as recalling a history of the place. So, too, the intriguingly shaped blocks of woodland in the Landschaftspark Riem in Munich by Latitude Nord, which are said to be "reminiscent of the historical field pattern",[41] are more eloquent of the designer's instinct for some dialogue between materials and geometry. By contrast, the elevated walkways built around the Roman Forum by the Nemesi Studio, while not landscape (although some archaeology and repaving took place), are intended to show off and help to interpret the buildings and remains of ancient Rome. History is enabled here, but its materials and narrative were already there and needed only to be observed.[42]

Unravelling layers of a site, even when, as at Barakaldo in Spain, they are actually laid out across the same surface, seems to be an appealing strategy, because such urban palimpsests seem to imply some historical awareness. The firm Gross.Max, as already cited, likes to appeal to what it calls an urban "strip tease"; so in

40 *Fieldwork*, pp.92–5.
41 Ibid, p.197
42 Ibid, pp.218–21.

94 History found and exploited in a specific place

transforming (or stripping away) the former maternity hospital in Glasgow, they retained a portico and retaining walls of white glazed bricks (very suggestive of such medical structures), and planted a square with snowdrops ("the emblem of the former hospital"); but otherwise the remembrance of the past is very faint. It did exploit the topography to great effect, and provides a great amenity, with trees and planting, fountains and a series of different terraces, set within the campus of the University of Strathclyde. But the historical effect will surely fade, like the winter snowdrops, and the jurors of European Foundation who hailed its "density of contextualism" (unless they really mean a range of spaces) seem off target.[43]

Attention to both ancient urban layouts or large areas of countryside can have more impact and sustain contexts. The Belgian city of Mechelen was once encircled by water, with a moat *inside* its fortifications. The moat was often used for dumping sewage or for washing (early buildings tended to back onto the water), and later was partly filled in or covered over (a not unfamiliar modern tactic in Belgian and Dutch cities with canals). So the OKRA landscape firm reopened over 300 metres of waterway. This move allowed the historical sense of the house alignments to be understood, while lining one side of the river Melaan with a double corridor for cars and parking and for pedestrians; but it is the texture of these zones – granite pavers, cobbles in the road, steel bridges to access the rear of the buildings – that draws quick attention to the mix of modern and old.[44]

A totally different response to the historical geography and use of the Swiss countryside in the Vaud, between the northern shore of Lac Léman and Lac de Neuchâtel to the north, was "to describe and codify the diversity of the canton's rural landscapes".[45] Here too the identification of typologies within this large area (3,000 square kilometres) helped to differentiate between the old and the necessarily new, allowing proposals to be made that offered "different scenarios leading to different futures". Not only did this study acknowledge dialogues between the older agricultural landscape and the new world of constructions and the infrastructure of roads, but it thereby was in a position to preserve and sustain a more ancient and beautiful landscape while still accepting development.

This large-scale attention to the relation of the old and the new is particularly useful when it comes to providing "gateways" – both literal and metaphorical – to important and long-established places or territories. Thresholds, small or large, alert visitors to some imminent encounter: as "in-between places they provide an opportunity for accommodation between adjoining worlds",[46] specifically between the historic and modern. This has attracted designers interested in large-scale infrastructure: the Seville airport is designed to lead visitors into the ancient city, even in the parking garage that refers to local historical forms – "patios with shades and open areas with orange trees", the deep blue arches and cupolas of the airport

43 *Fieldwork*, pp.136–9.
44 *On Site*, pp.118–21.
45 Ibid, pp.238–40. A similar approach was also made to the Veneto landscape (pp.242–7).
46 Kelly Shannon and Marcel Smets, *The Landscape of Contemporary Infrastructure*, p.140.

building itself, the blue-glazed roof tiles, and the exterior colouring of the concrete blocks.[47]

A totally different infrastructure is required when the landscape is both extensive, changing and constantly demanding. The Norwegian Tourist route project wants tourists to stop and admire the landscape along the 1,850 kilometres of its territory. Clearly this recalls the habit of identifying "stations" in picturesque experience around 1800, as the Norwegian route provides viewing platforms, walkways, and opportunities for photography. The insertions are deliberately modern – steel and glass – and elegantly detailed, and they are in explicit contrast with the enormous variety of the geological landscape, its fjords, waterfalls, coastal and mountain scenery. Here we have, as Shannon and Smets point out, a way of "staging" landscape history without unnecessarily intruding upon it other than by inserting places for viewing and contemplation.[48] And this staging or performance of the past has inspired some new approaches to such iconic places as the Mont St Michel.[49]

Historical reminiscences of plants, planting and garden forms

It is not surprising that garden forms (platforms and walkways, for example) and familiar plants recur in contemporary work; gardening practice has, after all, enjoyed a long-established tradition and the tools of its trade and its reliance on planting have not lapsed entirely but are constantly vivified. It is however odd that little is made of these references in the understanding and presentation of historical ground. Sometimes allusions to earlier garden forms – pergolas, screens, terracing, topiary even – seem innocent of any anterior motive; but recent efforts to make these elements dramatic and conspicuous – above all by the wit with which they are displayed, and by the use of unusual materials – have drawn attention to that role. Plants themselves can appeal to knowledgeable people, who can recognize the provenance of plants and can negotiate the Latin nomenclature that Linneaus or Jussieu bestowed on them. And the continuing presence of botanical gardens and arboreta, along with new examples established recently, continue to make available the historical past through an arsenal of garden materials and forms.

It is not surprising that many conceptualist "avant gardeners" (as Tim Richardson nicely terms them) play with both unusual forms and colours in gardens, even if the use to which they are put is traditional. Colour – not only in plants, but in the weird inscribing of coloured shapes as ground cover or to animate

---

47 Ibid, p. 37. Other sites of this sort are discussed on pp.36–ff, and the climbing escalators that conduct drivers from their parking up to the historic city of Toledo (pp.90–1).

48 Ibid, pp.130–1. But see also Janike Kampevold Larsen, "Geologic presence in a 21st-century wilderness garden", *Studies in the History of Gardens and Designed Landscapes*, 34/1 (2014), with its intriguing parallels between the Norwegian infrastructures and romantic Nordic paintings.

49 Ibid, pp.134–5.

96 History found and exploited in a specific place

standard items – is particularly insistent,[50] and it often highlights traditional manoeuvres that we have momentarily forgotten. Modern materials and their formats often remind one of how garden items used to be: if topiary was once clipped by gardeners into unusual shapes (unusual at least for the plant), then contemporary designers can manipulate plants on a variety of frames to mimic, say, antique clothing or sexual forms.[51] Hand-knitted nylon coloured carpets, along with zippers, are "soothing" in the Lullaby Garden in Sonoma, CA; wavy grass lawns preface a music school at Karlsruhe, Germany, or Dani Karavan heaves a line of white concrete waves across a lawn at Duisburg.[52] Gabions (small rocks and stones encased in wire) are part of a "Utility Garden" in Montreal, and a similar wall offers its ironic tribute to the many illegal immigrants who work the Californian vineyards and whose photographs are displayed on one of the wire screens.[53] Fountains are still much invoked, though nowadays usually recycled, which was not the case during the Renaissance; but they are also computerized, so that the water plays erratically, as at Parc André Citroën, and delight with their unpredictable sequence of displays. The designer Herbert Dreiseitl even uses water "as a design material": sheets of water make curtains, underlying surfaces make water ripple and play, though that had been done much earlier in the *catena d'acqua* at the Villa Lante, and wind and sounds animate his springs.[54] A water-purification park at Méry-sur-Oise by Pascal Cribier acknowledges the tradition of pools in French 17th-century gardens, yet edges of the pools are more mannerist, and the purified water sprays and emits mists mysteriously throughout the garden.[55] The hot-springs at Bad Oeynhausen in Westphalia shoot into the air, like fountains, but from within a steel and gabion-lined basin.[56] And when Garrett Eckbo designed the ALCOA garden for a firm of aluminium manufacturers, everything possible was contrived in that metal – screens, pergolas and an exotic fountain that itself mimicked a huge garden flower.[57] Whether these new materials imply or suggest

---

50 Martha Schwartz is particularly alert to the explosive elements of unexpected colour – see her Gifu Kitagata Apartments in Japan (*Avant Gardeners*, pp.260–1), but others have seized upon this exclamatory style, as in the pavement patterns by Susanne Burger (ibid, pp.54–7).

51 *Avant Gardeners*, pp.22–3, though these were designed for a garden show at Chaumont (see below in Chapter 7), that, as Richardson says, "brought out the best and worst in designers". Plant growth on steel skeletons is also well illustrated by Weilacher, *In Gardens*, pp.137–40.

52 *Avant Gardeners*, pp.62 and 161; for Duisburg, see *In Gardens*, p.67.

53 *Avant Gardeners*, pp.181 and 287; the latter was an installation at a garden festival, and clearly gabions are useful here, not least because such walls can be reused.

54 Ibid, pp.86–7. He has designed in a slightly more conventional way an impressive parkland at Tanner Springs, Portland, OR, where a palimpsestial strategy and title are invoked : see "Peeling back the surface: Portland's latest park gives functioning ecology and good urban design equal billing", *Landscape Architecture*, 96 (April, 2006), pp.112–19.

55 *Territories*, pp.62–5.

56 Ibid, pp.18–21.

57 See Marc Treib, *The Donnell and Eckbo Gardens* (San Francisco: William Stout, 2005), pp.98 ff.

History found and exploited in a specific place **97**

an obvious reworking of historic forms is unclear: the actual plants and uses of Eckbo's California garden were otherwise conventional.

The screen, divided into ten open rectangles, that Christopher Tunnard erected at the end of a terrace near Halland, Sussex, opens to a familiar English landscape[58]; this somewhat unusual (an ironic ?) use of a multiple picturesque viewing frame was reminiscent of the Renaissance device by which artists transcribed on a sheet of paper the object they were depicting through a squared frame (as in Dürer's *Underweysung der Messung*[59]). Habitual garden items – like walls – can be free-standing and unconnected, or fashioned in glass; planters – urban items in the spirit of Lawrence Halprin's familiar urban pots in concrete – take weird silicone shapes for Paula Hayes, or biodegradable plastic skins, both modernist 'takes' on the terracotta vases of Italian and arts and crafts gardens.[60] Contrariwise, geometry is revived, but offered conspicuously in studied formats, as if to draw attention to this surprising interest in gardenist formality.[61]

Vertical walls have become all the rage – and what were once planted parterres laid out on the ground are now hung on walls, while adding coolness and even climate control to their surroundings. These vertical gardens can also add a touch of whimsy – where tropical epiphytes and orchids that Ken Smith offers are "very much in contrast to the New York landscape", or Gross.Max's covering a tenement fire escape in London with plants that included "fireweed, which had thrived in building rubble after such disasters as the Great Fire of 1666 and the Blitz".[62] An instinct for humour is not a particularly marked characteristic among landscape architects, modern or in the past; yet the use of irony can bring out both historical and cultural elements in new design. To imitate the bespoke suits of British civil servants with "slightly eccentric or colourful linings", Neil Porter designed the Treasury courtyard with austere, clipped hedges and filled these "pocket" gardens with flowers, like silk handkerchiefs in breast pocket suits.[63] A bridge in Melbourne, Australia, was shaped by Arup engineers to mimic the woven-stick eel traps used by aborigines two centuries ago, and the two parts of a "mischievous" bridge in the Mur River in Graz, Austria, by the Acconci Studio, that connects a historical centre with a new neighbourhood, was formed as a dome that then metamorphosed into a bowl, both floating on a pontoon in the middle of a river. It certainly drew attention to a hitherto neglected and polluted

---

58 This is illustrated in Christopher Tunnard's *Gardens in the Modern Landscape* (Second, revised edition, London, 1948), p.68.

59 Illustrated in Anne Friedberg, *The Virtual Window* (Cambridge, MA: MIT Press, 2006), figure 1.5, with other examples shown in figures 1.7 and 1.8.

60 *Avant Gardeners*, pp.133–3, and 195.

61 Ibid, pp.181 and 287.

62 *Avant Gardeners*, pp.118 and 287. A very early patent for vertical wall installations was take out in 1938, and it is published by Richard L. Hindle, "A vertical garden: Origins of the vegetation-bearing architectural structure and system", *Studies in the History of Gardens and Designed Landscapes*, 32/2 (2012), pp.99–110.

63 *Avant Gardeners*, pp.126–7.

98 History found and exploited in a specific place

waterway; first used as a temporary performance space, it has now become a permanent fixture, and one hopes the pollution has abated.[64]

Surreal shapes inhabit the gardens of a state penitentiary near Utrecht, as if graffiti, coloured chalks and automatic writing had inscribed paths around about it.[65] In the office of a professional practice in Copenhagen, three different gardens play with conventional elements: scattered forms of geometry, paths that weave across lawns and even through hedges and screens, and large granite boulders scattered down a terraced walk of stairs.[66] But for those who did not recognize these moments as specifically historical were nevertheless – if unawares – finding themselves on fabricated ground. One of the more conspicuous modern design features seems to be a patchwork of different ground materials: maybe drawn from local sources and signalling local traditions – but the very patchwork effect draws attention to the one element of landscape architecture that one tends to take for granted.[67] The need to evade conventional forms on the ground, whether in paving or more extensively in planting beds, grass plots or pools of water, has produced an often dizzying, if not even confusing, appearance for visitors: these abstract forms are clearly responsive to the calls of modern art, as they imitate the work of Arp, Mondrian, Van Doesburg or Léger; but they also call attention to the historical forms that they are clearly seeking to avoid in early historical layouts.[68] The terraced lawns that descend like waves in a garden in Murten, Switzerland, by Günther Vogt, do – as Udo Weilacher notes, still "find their traditional models in the history of classical garden art", as do the contrasting materials of a box in an intricate parterre in the Swiss Center for Global Dialogue.[69] A well-head is perhaps unexpected in a courtyard of a Zürich office, as is the growth of moss, algae and lichen on the surrounding walls; but they are unsurprising in other contexts, and in a small intimate office space they recall some *hortus conclus* of mediaeval times, though again its modern austerity – the *sotto voce* feel in the space – is deliberate.[70]

Beyond the manipulation of landscape forms has come a renewed interest in the role of planting. A design by Piet Oudolf for the former sewage treatment plant at Bottrop, Germany,[71] parades a circular theatre of planting that, in its richness, reminds one of how we have lost a true sense of the resources of planting in an age much too dominated by a commercially produced, but limited, range of materials. A "theatre" of plants gave the title to John Parkinson's *Theatrum Botanicum* of 1640, signalling both the global reach of botanists and their wish to display or perform, as in a theatre, the riches discovered in new explorations. Parkinson's title page

---

64 *The Landscape of Comtemporary Infrastructure,* p. 218 and 172.
65 *Territories,* pp.44–5.
66 Ibid, pp.58–9.
67 See the examples illustrated in *Avant Gardeners,* pp.224–5 or 342–3.
68 I am thinking of the Interpolis Garden in Tilburg by WEST 8 (see *In Gardens,* pp.38–42).
69 Ibid, p.111 caption and p.115 for the parterre.
70 See figure 248 in my *A World of Gardens.* The *hortus conclusus* motif and even the term itself is taken up by Agence Ter for another garden, this time in Geneva.
71 See *Topos* (issue on "Culturescapes"), 78 (2012), p.59.

History found and exploited in a specific place **99**

actually shows a platform, as of the Globe theatre, on which Adam, the first gardener, and Solomon, the "scientist", are "performing". Now we have contemporary actors and botanical scientists on our own modern stages.

Botanical gardens and arboreta are indeed sites where the history of that science can be displayed or performed. It is also true that these places do not obviously suggest themselves as historical ground. Yet the use of Latin nomenclature suggests how plants acquired their names, and when the origins of plants are identified within botanical gardens, though the information is largely geographical, they could also recall how and when they came to be in this particular place. When the botanical garden is in a location originally designated and established as such – Padua, Pisa, Montpellier, Leiden, Oxford, Wellington (New Zealand), among others – part of its appeal is how long has been this historical search for plants and the wish to establish their significance and use. Arboreta, too, collect trees from all over the world: geographical first, but then, especially for the knowledgeable, a clue as to when and how long they have been here and whence they have come. Some trees, even outside arboreta, speak significantly of place and time. Lassus's plantings at Rochefort are a deliberate reminder of the source of the trees that arrived in France. Peter Walker's Keyaki Plaza in Saitama City, Japan, invoked the zelkova trees *(keyaki* in Japanese) and aligned them on a ceremonial route to a nearby shrine. For the Japanese, the allusion to both a historic temple, Hikawa, and the play with the name of both tree and city make sense; for the visitor, it is more the parade of trees and their wonderful mutations of colour in summer and autumn that give this place identity.[72] London plane trees, though used elsewhere, still conjure up memories of that city; cypresses, too, speak of Tuscany (even though a 19th-century fashion); rhododendra should recall the Himalayas, except they are everywhere these days and have lost – for most of us – their historical meaning. Indeed, one of the problems with using plants as markers of historical ground is that they are frequently the result of acclimatization or of hybridization and can no longer mark a historical moment; or we assume wrongly that a plant designates a vital moment in horticultural history, when it is in fact anachronistic.[73]

Knowledge of plants can make a considerable difference in the recognition of historical ground; yet it is, like geology, largely where an expert eye sees more than the casual observer. When Warren Byrd re-designed the Dell on the campus of the University of Virginia, he had several historical items to attend to, not least it being a campus designed by Thomas Jefferson: among his various responses was planting both magnolia Virginiana-Sweetbay (or Swamp Magnolia) and Magnolia tripetala (Umbrella magnolia) – yet it is only an expert eye that would recognize the first as

---

72 *Groundswell,* pp.58–63.
73 See Rebecca W. Bushnell's often hilarious account of recreations of "authentic" Elizabethan gardens, in "Gardens, Memory, and History", *Change over Time* (Spring, 2013), pp.64 ff. These include a rhododendron in an "Elizabethan" garden in Roanoke, VA, that was not introduced into England until much later (p.73).

100 History found and exploited in a specific place

a typical coastal plant, and the second being an upland/mountain variety. Yet this careful recognition of species reveals the site's topographical situation in Virginia.[74]

It can take something wonderful and unexpected to make plants read easily as a part of some historical ground. This was achieved by Laurie Olin in the garden forecourt of the Wexner Center for the Visual Arts in Columbus, OH, designed in collaboration with Peter Eisenman (Figure 5.15). His planting refers less to the immediate vicinity of the centre and its campus setting than to the plants of the eastern region of Ohio, and this range of reference probably allows more visitors to respond to its significance.[75] Transposing the prairie – its flatness, its regularity of the "Jeffersonian survey grid" and its seemingly endless landscape – seemed to Olin to evoke "the long-gone prairie". Yet this was not intended as mimicry, but rather as something "recreated", with many species of grass and native flowers, which overflow the planting boxes and appear to be spreading through the entry forecourt.

A similar excitement with the use of planting, and an insistence on recreation not mimicry, is found also at Dan Kiley's Fountain Place in Dallas (Figure 5.16). The plaza is enclosed by high bank buildings and hotels and provides a welcome respite from the climate, with a canopy of trees and with fountains descending and

FIGURE 5.15 Laurie Olin, drawing for the Wexner Center, The Ohio State University, Columbus, OH. (Courtesy of the artist).

74 Thanks to Warren Byrd for this information. See Linda McIntyre, "Making hydrology visible: The Dell, on the University of Virginia campus…", *Landscape Architecture,* 98 (August, 2008), pp.92–9, an essay that addresses how landscapers can make storm-water management both visible and beautiful, a topic discussed earlier in Chapter 2.
75 He addresses this theme more generally in his "Regionalism and the practice of Hanna/Olin, Ltd", *Regional Garden Design in the United States,* eds. Therese O'Malley and Marc Treib (Washington, DC: Dumbarton Oaks, 1995), pp.243–70. For an extensive analysis of this site see David Leatherbarrow, *Topographical Stories,* pp.236–48.

FIGURE 5.16 Dan Kiley, Fountain Place, Dallas, Texas.

splashing down its length.[76] One of Kiley's remarks upon seeing the original site was to say that he wanted an "urban swamp", an impression that does not seem to fit this city site or perhaps appeal to its average visitor or local business people: nor do the wonderful descending levels of water replicate anything I envisage as a swamp. Yet when a Texan student of mine produced his own photograph of a Texan swamp, it made Kiley's remark and the ultimate design more plausible; especially as the trees that Kiley inserted in the circular planting pods, around which the flowing waters bubble and splash, are bald cypresses. And Kiley himself wrote that his design, rather than mimic some real swampland, was to be "a compacted experience of nature so intense that it would be almost super-natural". It is a wonderful oasis, and the plants, whether we recognize the cypresses immediately or not, suggest a place that fakes a plausible if "super-natural" habitat for human consumption.

Botanical gardens continue to suggest how much we relish their collections and presentations. This is undoubtedly because people like to see plants close-up, "codified" and explained, and can learn how to use them in their own gardens; but they also often reveal a dedication to the past – noticing how plants have grown, recognizing earlier discoveries of new species, acknowledging the claims of past

---

76 Dan Kiley and Jame Amidon, *Dan Kiley: The complete Works of America's Master Landscape Architect* (Boston, MA: Little, Brown and Company, 1999), pp.98–105. Quotations taken from this text.

102 History found and exploited in a specific place

collectors and regimes (the Medici in Italy, or the amateurs of the Royal Society in England). But like so much historical ground they prepare the future (almost literally) for horticulture, as plants are secured and developed for later generations. New botanical gardens respond both to the previous ways of presenting material, but, being modern gardens, stake claims upon the present and future with new designs. Two new sites in France and China make this clear.

If modern botanical gardens offer the same appeal as earlier ones, their forms rarely mimic older sites, although the need to provide individual compartments for the cultivation and scrutiny of distinct plants and species largely determines their format. The large Chenshan Botanical Garden at Shanghai (200 hectares) was started in 2007 and completed three years later.[77] It is designed both for its amenities as a public park and for the display of its plants and ecosystems in the garden and in the long, low greenhouses and research building at the edge of the site. It contains fairly extensive compartments for display in 35 themed gardens – anemones, roses, the flowering osmanthus (barely known in Europe and associated with the Chinese Moon festivals, and displayed here in its various forms of trees and shrubs), ferns and riparian plants, irises for moist and dry locations (a spectrum of colours like the rainbow), and water gardens in a series of small rectangular pools. Bamboo is everywhere. Some areas display oil-producing plants, vegetables, "biogas plants" to demonstrate the importance of energy crops, or medical plants (a strong historical emphasis in Chinese medicine). All these are arranged (even in the water garden) within irregularly shaped, sculptural forms, rising like islands in the wetlands (a possible allusion to the local landscape that existed many years before); the site as a whole is contained with an irregular ring of embankments, avoiding straight lines and evidence of geometry.

The size, at least on a brief visit, is somewhat defeating, not least because of this profusion of irregular forms. Yet this garden also responds, even within this obviously deliberate modern display of geographical and historical botany, with a keen sense of Chinese garden traditions: flowers are less important than the landscape, which must represent the larger world of "mountains and valleys, water and rocks, desert and forest, shadows and light", all within the irregular enclosure of the perimeter embankments. Hence the traditional Chinese insistence on water and mountain. Water is everywhere – and the barges that ply the canals in the vicinity will eventually be admitted into the garden waterways. Through a passage cut into the large hill, visitors descend to the water level in an old stone quarry (Figure 5.17), where they walk on pontoons or "swinging bridges" beneath the hanging rocks of the quarry walls (again, a gesture to old Chinese engravings). Its artifice is, nonetheless, in keeping with long traditions of Chinese gardening – the sense of an apparently natural landscape is mediated by carefully contrived forms.

---

77 Donata and Christoph Valentien, *Shanghai New Botanical Garden* (Berlin: Jovis Verlag, 2008), by the authors of the planning group for the site. That this garden also seems to suggest something of a garden festival may not be entirely incidental (see below, in Chapter Seven).

FIGURE 5.17 The flooded quarry in the Shanghai Botanical Gardens (Photo: Emily T. Cooperman).

It is this emphasis, as Donata & Christoph Valenten explain, that allows them to represent Shanghai's botanical park as both "another time, [and] a new understanding".

Catherine Mosbach's botanical gardens at Bordeaux (Figure 5.18), another design constructed on a former industrial riverside between 1997 and 2007, deploys one of the standard formats for displaying plants in small, segregated and identifiable areas. It continues the old functions of a botanical garden as a research institute, but its straightened format – a long space 2,000 by 230 feet – is marshalled into a series of very unusual gardens: a water garden, an "Environment Garden" and a Field of Crops, which together represent the "characteristics of the surrounding Aquitaine Basin".[78] In the Environment Garden eleven randomly shaped segments provide different habitats, where visitors can see the variety of materials and topographical elements in raised compartments (grassy dunes, dry prairie, etc.). In contrast, the Field of Crops is strictly geometrical, each long zone a different system, separately irrigated. Those plots exaggerate the conventional beds of older botanical gardens like those at Pisa or Padua, while around the large water basin at one end of the site, a series of small aquatic water tanks, quadrilateral and variously rhomboid, are strikingly unusual and draw attention to the modernity of this long established garden type.

78 *Groundswell*, pp.84–9, quoted here from p.84. But see further in Mosbach's *Traversées/Crossings* (Paris: ICI Interface, 2010), pp.62–75, and *Fieldwork*, pp.106–11.

FIGURE 5.18 Catherine Mosbach, the Botanical Garden at Bordeaux, France (Photo: Emily T. Cooperman).

There are many contemporary designs for which references or allusions to older garden forms have been used; most are deliberate, but not all make their way beyond the designer and are available to those who use and respond to these spaces. For the Shenzhen Stock Exchange, Inside Outside chose distinct "traditional gardens" of squared flower beds but juxtaposed and referenced them to Chinese forms.[79] We see the modernity, the new-fangleness,[80] of the spaces at Bordeaux or Shanghai, but not necessarily that they derive from earlier forms. The odd line of what appear to be grottoes down one side of Parc André Citroën, or the blocks of stone from which spout the "sources" of rivers in another part of that site, are not clearly gestures to historical garden making. Yet everywhere in modern place-making there are pergolas, screens, fountains, gardens compartments, grottoes and elegant double staircases as codified by Serlio, with a concave set of steps crossing a small circular platform to descend down further, but now convex, stairs.[81] Many

---

79 *LOTUS international*, 150 (2012), pp.32–5.
80 This is not an insult: I borrow the word from the Elizabethan translator of Castiglione's *The Courtier* when he struggled to find a modern English word for the Italian "spezzatura", which we might translate better as spontaneity or studied nonchalance.
81 Serlio derived his stairs from what Bramante designed at the Belvedere at the Vatican, and he in his turn took the form from a Roman temple: it was much involved in arts and crafts gardens, and a version of the same form greets one at an entrance to the Tate Gallery in London.

garden centres cater precisely for those who wish to invoke historical forms and events like garden seats, fountains (especially small Japanese devices – *shishi-odoshi* or deer scarers), Japanese lanterns, terracotta vases (often in plastic), reproductions (miniaturized usually) of classical deities. Personal, private gardens perform largely or solely for their owners, though their forms and materials may rely necessarily on past design practice; their histories are otherwise occluded if not, in fact, left to their owners to invest with whatever freightage, historical, social or idiosyncratic, they desire. Where we will find a concerted meditation on the forms and meanings of garden traditions is in the garden festivals and horticultural exhibitions – and these are taken up later in Chapter Seven.

6

HISTORY "INVENTED" FOR A SITE TODAY

"gardens have almost always foretold in advance the relationships between man and nature, and between society and nature"

(Bernard Lassus)[1]

The question, Bernard Lassus pondered, is "What is the time of a garden?".[2] He was not talking about the obvious "time" of a garden – its seasonal rhythm or the hours of the day, but about how we might envisage historical time ("le temps") of a garden. The occasion was his decision *not* to intervene in an old and somewhat abandoned garden at the Chateau de Barbirey-sur-Ouche, Burgundy, in 1996; but instead, to engrave, upon the windows that looked out upon it, images from the years around 1900, along with other recollections of how former gardens might have looked. So the garden has a past, but it also (when the trees outside grow old and die) has a future: "how can we imagine, in the face of the present, the changes that may take place, or indeed a past existence that might have come to pass?" It was, a game (*jeu*) for the garden[3] (Figure 6.1).

Yet, as games can also be serious, this one played with the spatial and temporal event of the garden: it asked how we might invent a garden. Gazing at the unkempt garden through glass, on which were engraved past images of careful topiary, strange carvings of tree stumps, a garden *fabrique* and a cluster of pine trees, our gaze was interrupted and our imagination provoked: the images on the glass were close to the spectator, but far from him in time; whereas what was outside the window (there were, after all, 'French windows') was far in space, but close in time (the garden now). In historical terms, the garden out there was real and present, but also

1   *The Landscape Architecture of Bernard Lassus,* p.116.
2   See Stephen Bann's account of this project, ibid, pp.35–41.
3   Lassus handed out a text entitled "Le jeu du jardin, mode d'emploi" at the time of his "intervention" on the site.

History "invented" for site today **107**

FIGURE 6.1 Garden games of Bernard Lassus, Chateau de Barbirey-sur-Ouche, Burgundy, France. (Photo courtesy of the designer).

accessible only through our imagination and the images that prompted it. That was the intervention.

A middle ground

In discussions of historical ground there are what we might call "grey" areas, sites that fall neither into the category of history found and exploited in a specific place nor of those that are wholly invented. When Georges Descombes explained his "attitude towards intervening in the landscape", it involved circling "around [and] paying attention to that which one would like to be present where no one expects it any more. Thus, for me, to recover something – a site, a place, a history, or an idea – entails a shift in expectation and point of view".[4] He was never, he says, "particularly interested in reconstructing a historical lineage"; indeed, his concern was to recognize "changes in time". So he wishes for "a precision of disposition, articulation, arrangement … so that a pre-existing place can be found, disturbed, awakened and brought to presence".

4 "Shifting Sites…", in *Recovering Landscapes: Essays in Contemporary Landscape Architecture,* ed. James Corner (New York: Princeton Architectural Press, 1999), pp.79–80. See also Georges Descombes, "Wanderweg mit Akzenten – Looking to the past – the Swiss Path", *Topos,* 3 (May 1993), pp.93–9, also the essay by F. Morin *et al.,* in *Spazio e società,* 15/57 (Jan–March 1992). The whole project, discussed in the following paragraph, was eventually abandoned, but this Geneva stretch was published, illustrated and with contributions by various authors, as *Voie Suisse: L'itineraire genevois de Morschach à Brunnen* (Geneva, Switzerland: Médecine & Hygiene, 1991).

108 History "invented" for site today

This concept he took up when he contributed to the Swiss Path around Lake Uri, designed to celebrate the 700th Anniversary of the Swiss Confederation, with each canton taking on a segment of the route around the lake; Descombes took the 2-kilometre stretch from Morshach to Brunnen. Drawing on historical Siegfried maps in six editions from 1894 to1947, it was clear that the path had been subject to alteration for over a hundred years. The idea now was to make the history of the various routes "visible", to reveal the path's potential once again, drawing attention to its long existence without major interventions, yet at the same time to generate "a feeling of oddness, creating a source of different attention, a different vision, a different emotion". Walking the path was a means of responding to what was there through careful, subtle highlighting of elements along its route – the streams that crossed it, the flora of the forest, its ecology. Any obtrusive and confusing items, "kitsch constructions" or studied picturesque "stations", were removed, but without losing view sheds or making the route unsafe. Glacial boulders were "cleaned" of grass and lichen to reveal the white rock and to make visitors notice the random scattering of these erratics. Some edges of paths were reinforced, but with concrete or other modern materials; railings were replaced with galvanized tubing, wooden steps with metal strips. These left "a mark of our own time, to overlay an unequivocal trace" of contemporary activity.

Two other bigger moves were to respond to the incidence of an old railway line and link it to the path that passed below it; wooden steps up the slope joined them, but could also be used as seats to take in the view. More visibly, a steel belvedere, the *Chanzeli* (Figure 6.2), 16 meters in diameter and 9 tall, was placed high above the lake: its metallic structure contrasted with the forest, but through its open and circular form the landscape all around could still be viewed. Now a belvedere is a quintessential 19th-century feature, the sort that allowed tourists to observe the scenery comfortably and to admire the "beautiful view".[5] But another Swiss designer, Paolo Bürgi, who had also sought to avoid a too easy touristic experience, pushed his promenade out over the tree tops at Cardada. Descombes, too, wanted to frustrate a conventional response by improving on how the Swiss landscape could be viewed today, shifting our usual expectations; so he cut what he called a "postcard" opening in the curved front of the belvedere, and with this mildly ironic gesture, combined with taking in a 360-degree survey of the landscape from within its open structure, he welcomed a historical experience within a palpably contemporary moment.

One further intervention was made, not on the land but in a book, that addressed the afterlife of the design: visitors might lead themselves along the path by using the book faithfully; others would ignore it completely, while others would

---

5   A similar belvedere was similarly projected by Paolo Bürgi, for the Castellazzo Doberdò; in this unfamiliar and extraordinary landscape, a path is cut through two karstic walls, where the visitor gets to touch and see, close-up, the geology, and then proceeds to the belvedere and views the lake below. See Paolo Bürgi, *Paesaggi-Passaggi,* introduced by Carlo Magnani (Melfi, Italy: Casa Editrice Libria, 2011), p.147.

FIGURE 6.2 Georges Descombes, the Chanzeli on the the Swiss Path, Lake Uri, Switzerland.

know about this Swiss path only through the book. So the genius of place reveals itself in a variety of mediations – by a direct exploration of the path, indirectly through reading the book, and in a middle way by mixing the two, understanding the historical ground in its modern formulation.

Bringing a place "to presence" (Descombes' phrase) pertains as much to inventing a site as to recollecting what had been there. So there is, certainly, a grey area between these two. The American landscape architect George Hargreaves seems to exemplify this middle position. Suspicious of both words and theory, he has let other critics comment upon what he does. But he does himself briefly address a situation where, as he cannot rely on "underlying conditions, what I like to call good bones" (the geology and topography examined in Chapter Two), his work must confront sites to "create bones where there are none".[6] He is keen to emphasize that "narratives" are formed by site histories and to invoke what he calls "time", though this is less deep time than how contemporary cultural and historical events – recreation, festivals, performances, gardens – might impact the finished work (p.6). He is intrigued with the "longevity of public spaces", what he calls locality or "identity" (the old *genius loci* re-invented perhaps).

The overall effect of so many of his projects is indeed of narrative, not only fabricated for the site, but exaggerated, so that those histories can be grasped, like

6 *Landscape Alchemy. The work of George Hargreaves,* with contributions by George Hargreaves, Julia Czerniak, Anita Berrizbeitia and Liz Campbell Kelly (Novato, CA: ORO Editions, 2009), p.6.

110 History "invented" for site today

the cluster of five mounds at a water treatment plant, the Brightwater Mitigation Area in Washington State, where, by taking a trail of bridges and overlooks, you can understand the system.[7] While the underlying rationale of his work may be, as his commentators like to point out, complex and intricate, the "experience" of place is frequently bold and even unsubtle. This seems, in fact, a valuable instinct, because it moves projects beyond professional concerns and into a more open, general and accessible public realm. This does not mean that we are invited to exist only at that level, but by first responding to a site that way, we graduate to a larger and perhaps more complex picture.[8] A park should be, he writes, "special to the individual in their experience of the moment", while being at the same time "part of a collective consciousness": this ambition to maintain a balance between the individual and the crowd, between the immediately graspable and deeper, more scientific intentions, is hard to maintain today; but it is also essential. Visitors must be "able to decipher how the landscape reads within its context", so "legibility" is the key ingredient of his work.[9]

And just as Hargreaves wishes for a public that is capable of "reading" a site, so he also counts upon its "durability": because, however much professionals can maintain and nurture a site after it has been established, it is non-professionals, above all visitors, who will in fact use and manage it over the long term. He envisages the stages by which the London Olympic ground could be transformed from its "games mode" to a place where fewer crowds will respond to a less busy parkland. And for Los Angeles State Park he "anticipates a *future* of rich urban open space and a reclaimed relationship to its natural systems"[10] by phasing the planting as three distinct modes, from native, pre-settlement species, to colonial plantings, and eventually to ceremonial and cultural gardens. This progress through historical manipulations will change, for its future is open: does the city absorb the landscape in some form (almost certainly), or (less likely) can the recovered river's edge win over more of the parkland? Hargreaves is particularly alert to this gradation of plant forms and uses, and at the Shelby Farms, in Memphis, he specifically honours the dialogue between farmed land and consciously designed spaces for aesthetic pleasure.[11]

---

7   This attention to how narratives in landscape can be seen and understood by its users was also noticed in the discussion of storm-water management in Chapter Two.
8   I am in a way complaining that too many landscape critics, theorists especially, go straight to a complex and even complicated view that leaves all but the professionals behind. That will never get landscape architecture the attention it deserves from a wider public, who need to understand these things.
9   All these references and that in the paragraph that follows are from *Landscape Alchemy*, p.7.
10 Ibid, pp.222–37 and 220 (my italics).
11 He also draws upon my own triad of natures (untouched, culturated, designed), cited on p.220; but he misses at Shelby Farms the work of Garrett Eckbo, whose contribution to this dialogue between second and third nature was briefly noted in the second edition of Christopher Tunnard's *Gardens in the Modern Landscape* (London, UK: The Architectural Press, 1948), p.142, illustrating community gardens, as they were then called.

History "invented" for site today **111**

What may seem, in photographs, computer drawings or plans of Hargreaves' work, merely eccentric and conspicuous items, make superb sense on the ground – the telegraph poles, the earthworks and the chevrons at Byxbee Field define and mark out the ground (shades perhaps of Wallace Stevens' music at Key West, where a song "mastered the night and portioned out the sea"). The elaborate edges and markings of his waterfronts at Chattanooga, TN, New Orleans, and San Francisco, or the intricacies of pathways for the University of Cincinnati campus green with its levels and fountains, all draw attention to the site and help it perform for visitors. So do his fountains, which are inventive, modern and speak to their location. With his signature mounds, elliptical berms and fragmented geometrical references he is, self-confessedly, in debt to land artists. Yet while Robert Smithson, Walter de Maria and Richard Serra may certainly be his sources, and behind them the serpent mounds of Native American culture, he translates them into lived and *usable* space.[12] The folded ridges of the Clinton Presidential Center Park (Figure 6.3), or the Japanese-like horse-shoe references to Zen gardens at the National Museum of Emerging Science and Innovation in Tokyo are spaces that are accessible and we can inhabit; the tall columns of lights along the Atlantic Ocean at South Pointe Park in Miami Beach, or the phone poles at Byxbee may recall Walter de Maria's Lightning Field, but we move and walk between them and know the place by our movement through it. It might insult him to say his work is picturesque (because

FIGURE 6.3 George Hargreaves, folded ridges at the Clinton Presidential Center, Little Rock, Arkansas. (Photo: John Gollings).

12 I take this up in a final essay here, where land art's contribution to historical ground is explored.

112 History "invented" for site today

that habitual term is moribund), but if we accept that movement of both feet and mind was the essence of the original picturesque, Hargreaves is frequently and absorbingly picturesque.[13]

Anita Berrizbeitia[14] has invoked the idea of the palimpsest as one key word of Hargreaves' conceptual thinking: yet that term has even wider relevance than she allows – for it copes with combinations of different ground conditions and insertions, and levels of meaning. As such, her sense of palimpsest has more affinities with Genette than with a manuscript palimpsest. The latter often needs some skill at recovering earlier layers (think of the Archimedes project), whereas much of Genette's paratextuality is more obvious: Joyce's *Ulysses* clearly gestures to Homer, even if the intricacies of this parallel are in need of uncovering. The claim that Hargreaves work looks "'natural' to the untrained eye", but is in fact not meant to signify "nature",[15] is of a piece with Genette's palimpsest, which values allusion or citation, even plagiarism. Thus for the Louisville Riverfront Park, in Kentucky, Hargreaves juxtaposes a variety of landscape topologies (marina, play areas, lawns, riparian edges) that overlap less than they gesture to different readings of a large site (Figure 6.4). Similarly, he can conceive for the Hudson Park and Boulevard in New York a variety of historical ecologies that recall landscapes of Manhattan before it was settled: episodes of Chestnut-Tulip Forest, Pine Barrens, native grasslands, and a fountain springing up (wittily) where the modern subway emerges onto 34th Street. Into these segments he also inserts layers of different "programs" (café, dog park, children's playground).[16] And if Hargreaves' palimpsests rescue elements of the past, they also gesture to the future: ensuring that future developments are not preempted by the immediate design, but manage possible changes over a long time; they may even – as in the case of parchment – be scraped and reused at a later date.

Maybe other designers occupy this same middle ground between feigned and true historical ground; or occupy a shifting and moveable ground between them. Like many reformulations of industrial or derelict land, the Parque del Clot in Barcelona (Figure 6.5)[17] melds bits of old history with a new confection, and at the same time it sits somewhere between being a square (in the southern half of the space) or a small park (in the north). Between 1985 and 1986 the remains of a

---

13 See John Dixon Hunt, "John Ruskin, Claude Lorrain, Robert Smithson, Christopher Tunnard, Nikolaus Pevsner, and Yve-Alain Bois walked into a bar...", *The Hopkins Review* (new series), V.2 (2012).

14 *Landscape Alchemy,* p. 63: she takes the term from his second essay published in that volume. Her essay draws upon two essays Hargreaves wrote: "Post Modernism Looks Beyond itself", *Landscape Architecture* (1983), pp.60–5, and "Large Parks: a Designer's Perspective", in *Large Parks,* ed. Julia Czerniak and George Hargreaves (New York, 2007), pp.121–73.

15 Ibid, p.62.

16 Ibid. pp.278–85, among his competitions.

17 *In Gardens,* pp.164–8. The Parque del Clot seems to bring within its enclosure a wealth of opportunities that suggest a Genette-like palimpsest of allusions, quotations and plagiarisms

History "invented" for site today 113

FIGURE 6.4 George Hargreaves, Louisville Riverfont Park, Kentucky. (Photo: John Gollings).

FIGURE 6.5 Parque del Clot, Barcelona, Spain. (Photo courtesy of Udo Weilacher).

114 History "invented" for site today

former railway workshop were metamorphosed into a strange, almost theatrical setting of arcades that resemble an aqueduct (there is still a ribbon of water along its summit until it falls into a pool below), a generous flight of steps, a sunken pool, a cluster of arches that formerly held up the roof of a factory hall but now sits like some Islamic hallway, with a small pool, open to the skies and drooping with vines; over it all towers an immensely tall factory chimney. Within the smallish space of the Parc is included a great variety of opportunities, from a children's playground, a ball park, to the semblance of a lavish natural landscape and a romantic ruinscape. This site has become both a much respected example of how to respond to an honoured past and how a vibrant future can be achieved.

Bernard Lassus figures in any discussion of history in the modern garden, not least because he is a dedicated modernist. For, as a good modernist, he is alert to the precedents and past modes that will sustain his own best work; for gardens, he notes, "have almost always foretold in advance the relationships between ... society and nature".[18]

Two of his unrealised projects use the habits of some cultural past to suggest a new sense of today. Wells are a familiar item in countries where water was, or still is, drawn from below ground, and a familiar childhood pastime is to drop pebbles into them to hear them ring at the bottom and to guess how deep they are. But at the University of Montpellier, the stones would either fall "forever" (captured by a foam bottom that absorbed the sound), or if the pebbles hit protuberances down the sides of the well shaft, streams or springs of water were released.[19] The habit of sensing time by the time the stone takes to drop, is unexpectedly revised, as is the sense that water may gush below but it not be drawn up to the surface. Similarly, for a projected park outside a new town of L'Isle d'Abeau, Lassus wished to keep its imagined "past" alive by inventing for it a pond in which an earlier village had been submerged. Within its depths was the "lost" or drowned village of olden times (hence the "Garden of the Anterior"[20]). Wandering beside the pond, we might hear the "tolling bells" of the Lac du Bar emerging from the waters, or by gazing into columns or inverted periscopes discover "micro-landscapes" in the depths below (drowned landscapes of The Enchanted Tree, or the Grotte de la Bonne Femme....).

When he designs gardens for a new corporate HQ in the Parisian suburb of Boulogne-Billancourt (a building designed by Pierre Riboulet), the place does not elicit any strong historical interest (with one exception in the general area, to which I'll come). So Lassus invents a variety of different gardens, which themselves refer to a whole history of garden design: a garden of the seasons that acts as a reception terrace for the HQ, a garden of pines for the staff ("hommage à Francis Ponge"), a balcony (Le Jardin de l'Attente) and a private garden for the CEO on the top of the building, a so-called green theatre (Jardin de Verdure). Together they

18 *The Landscape Approach of Bernard Lassus*, p.116.
19 *The Landscape Approach*, p.25.
20 *Antérieur* here meaning earlier, or of the past. Ibid, pp.110–15.

History "invented" for site today **115**

constitute the "hanging gardens" of COLAS.[21] Yet each element, while still acknowledging familiar precedents, extends its gardenist vocabulary (Figure 6.6).

The ground floor reception terrace, designed to welcome visitors for "les cocktails" is a wooden terrace, that has nonetheless all the other necessary accoutrements of a small intimate garden: there is an outer ring of real bushes that screen the road outside, but in front of them are both a hedge performed in steel laser cut-outs and trees, also in steel cut-out, that rise now from a low shrubbery of actual boxwood that sits likewise in perforated steel trays. On the other side of the wooden boards of the "garden" are three "flowerbeds", the flowers being clusters of plastic balls on sticks. On another side of the garden is a fountain, splashing real water (re-circulating) that runs down innumerable small teak cups in the form of an Islamic *chadar*, and serves to mitigate sounds from the street outside.

FIGURE 6.6 Bernard Lassus, the reception "garden" at COLAS HQ, Paris.

21 Bernard Lassus and other contributors, *Les Jardins Suspendus de COLAS*, privately printed for Colas S.A. and Lassus, Paris (c.2008). Lassus has used "artificial bushes" composed of multi-coloured enamel balls in earlier interventions, as at the school building at Guénange in Lorraine, or steel representations of foliage for the Square Damia in the 11th arrondissement of Paris; but at COLAS the effect is much more insistent. See Michel Conan, "'The Gardens of Seasons' by Bernard Lassus: Coming to terms with fleeting encounters in a decentered world", *Contemporary Garden Aesthetics, Creations and Interpretations*, ed. Michel Conan (Washington DC: Dumbarton Oaks, 2007), pp.97–119. See my forthcoming essay on "Bernard Lassus and the varieties of nature", forthcoming in a yet untitled volume, ed. Annette Fiero.

116 History "invented" for site today

The garden thus mixes growing and metal plants: but the free-standing "trees" are changed appropriately to reflect the colours of each season, and the flower beds could be moved around and "replanted".

This repertoire is resumed, variously, on the higher levels. Flowerbeds on the upper floor for the CEO are now provided with detachable and moveable items, so that we can "pick" the flowers, "transplant" or "dead-head" them. Yet the pine gardens for the staff on a series of balconies are filled with miniature pine bushes set in brown stones, but also within steel cut-out planters. This garden further alludes (in the manner of Genette) to the poet Francis Ponge, the supreme poet of "things", whose writings about landscape, weather, seasons and meadows are paratextualized. In particular, Lassus seems to invoke Ponge's "Bois des Pins": citing "Evolutions à pied faciles entre ces grands mâts nègres ou tout au moins creoles, encortiqués encore et lichéneux jusques à mi-hauteur, graves comme le bronze, souples comme le caoutchouc" (moving easily over large black or at least creole mats, but waxed and covered with lichen to mid-height, grave as bronze, supple as India-rubber).[22]

The CEO's garden is the least attentive to natural planting: descending from the Jardin de l'Attente (a platform or "waiting" room), we reach a space in the form of a green theatre (a conventional historical format for baroque gardens); but this is entirely constructed in elaborately cut, steel "foliage", perforated sheets that convey, magically as elsewhere, the density of natural forms; the theatre also takes the shape of a theatre with wings (*coulisses*), and we move through these openings onto the back "stage" that narrows and vanishes towards a recess that contains a computer, where – in another conventional picturesque moment – we see distant images of an waterfall, but now abstracted on a screen; after dark, its falling waters gleam brightly at the back of the theatre.

This is, obviously, a wholly modern garden, but it is a modern garden clearly inspired by former devices and expectations about garden use, even if here and now it presents itself in the starkly metallic forms of today. These past forms and ideas foretell how contemporary gardens might be renewed. It is, too – apart from the ground floor reception area – a series of roof gardens, with recollections (paratexts) of the hanging gardens of Babylon, descending terraces in Italian Renaissance villas, or Le Corbusier's listing of roof gardens as the second of *Les 5 points d'une architecture nouvelle* in 1926 (Corbu also built in Boulogne-Billancourt, so the historical gesture is well-taken).

True invention and a "most feigning" history

Here the issue is, paradoxically, whether we can notice that some design feigns or invents history for a site, yet still can accept that it is, or could be, true in that place.

---

22 Quoted by Lassus in his *Couleur, lumière, paysage: Instants d'une pédagogie* (Paris: Momum. Editions du Patrimonie, 2004), p.88, citing Ponge's *Oeuvres completes*, (Paris: Galimard, 1993), vol. 2, p.105. Ponge's "encortiqués" is perhaps a neologism for "encaustiguer".

And that judgement must ultimately reside with the user; as Arthur Danto insisted, artworks require interpretation – to be interpreted is their essence.[23] Nonetheless, good landscape designs clearly reach out for an understanding visitor who will accept both the truth *and* the invention, and perhaps work to comprehend what is not, on the surface, always clear-cut; good gardens require work from their creator and from those who visit them.

A striking example of a garden that cries out for "interpretation", which is also truly feigned and yet seems to be an interesting instance of history crafted for a site that possessed none (or at least none of the "history" that can now be found there), is the Garden of Cosmic Speculation. Devised and designed by Charles Jencks and his late wife, Maggie Keswick, the ground is attached to the site of a house in Lowland Scotland, Portrack, itself an interesting, architectural mixture of Georgian architecture with Victorian picturesque (white walls and black pointed roofs). It takes its name from a ruined castle, the remains of which are somewhere on the site, and which guarded, probably since Roman times, a ford over the adjacent River Nith. Portrack's mid-20th-century garden was an artful and "crafted wilderness" dense with shrubs, trees and scented flowers; a true "English" (or Scots) gardener's garden. Yet what was then crafted elsewhere in this landscape undertakes a totally different history, a speculative narrative of the cosmos.

Visitors who know nothing of the site before their visit (which must be hard, as few would probably stumble upon it unawares), or who do not recall the insights or information provided by Jencks's own book on the garden[24] will be confronted with an astonishing and rich assemblage of forms: lakes and streams, a bridge, stepping stones across a river, stairways or terraces, sculptured mounds, *fabriques* or follies (an octagon; a "Nonsense" building), enclosed gardens, a wonderful anthology of gates and doorways, finials, seats, greenhouses – in short, a compact history in itself of garden elements and devices. But few of these, if any, will strike a visitor as familiar, simply because in each case the garden proffers them in unusual ways. The bridge is twisted or "jumping", fractals that tilt against each other (Figure 6.7); the striking stairway or descending terrace from the house is an interlacing zigzag of white blocks that cross and re-cross each other before merging into a single stairway that descends into a pond; the parterres of the enclosed garden, richly embroidered, feature strange emblems at the centre of each square; "terraces" are like chessboards, but warped and bent; the iron gates whirl and metamorphose (Figure 6.8). Everywhere are "waves, twists and folds", images of complexity that organize water, soil and weather, labyrinthine forms, recent discoveries of cosmology. Visitors will need to recognize some of the embedded references –

23 Arthur Danto, *The Transfiguration of the Commonplace: A Philosophy of Art* (Cambridge, MA: Harvard University Press, 1981), p.125.
24 Jencks has written an absorbing and indeed exhaustive (even a touch exhausting) book on the site, *The Garden of Cosmic Speculation* (London: Frances Lincoln, 2003), and I make no attempt to retell that narrative; instead I want to look to the matter of its feigned history and how it may be registered. All quotations in my text are from his book.

118 History "invented" for site today

FIGURE 6.7 The Garden of Cosmic Speculation, Portrack House, near Dumfries in South West Scotland. The Jumping Bridge. (Courtesy of Charles Jencks).

Möbius strips, DNA symbols – and be alert at the very least to current ideas in chaos theory and fractals. So much is demanded of them.

    Now all of those ideas are maybe confirmed by a "certain slowing of time", as we wander and absorb the garden; for this is not a place to rush through and gape. But the descriptions in the paragraph above are plucked from the captions affixed to the five double-page photographs that open Jencks's book, which function as visual prolegomena for the textual analyses that follow. There is therefore a sense in which we need our experiences of the garden before we enter into the book and its narratives. First, we need both the sheer excitement and bafflement of the garden forms to send us back to the book's account of the garden that follows those tantalizing five images; but then we must return to the garden once more, and probably many times.

History "invented" for site today **119**

FIGURE 6.8 The Garden of Cosmic Speculation, Portrack House, near Dumfries in South West Scotland. The Soliton Waves gate. (Courtesy of Charles Jencks).

For we have lost the habit of "reading" complex gardens that humanists like Pirro Ligorio at Villa d'Este, learned literati in the woods of Bomarzo, or learned academicians at Versailles might have counted on; such knowledgeable security of interpretation, available to the well-educated, was beginning to fade quickly by the middle of the 18th century – at least in the United Kingdom.[25] And we have also, unless we are lucky as well as persistent, small chance of endlessly frequenting a particular landscape until it absorbs our whole imagination (unlike the chance of re-reading a book, listening to a piece of music again and again, or seeing a play many times). That is the afterlife of any work of art, but it is more difficult to achieve in designed landscapes.

That said, it is hard to respond to the Garden of Cosmic Speculation on the basis of one lengthy visit, since it cries out (according to Danto, and Jencks himself) for "interpretation". But one thing is certain – this garden may use symbols, but they are not allegorical; there is no one-for-one equation of items in the garden with ideas from physics. Allegory might be "restful", as Jane Gillette argues,[26] but the Garden of Cosmic Speculation is anything but restful and is not allegorical. Not least because it disturbs, affronts us and puzzles us with its imagery and how we connect those with our larger ideas from "outside the garden". Jencks's book is

25 See my essay "Stourhead revisited and the pursuit of meaning in gardens", *Studies in the History of Gardens and Designed Landscapes*, 26/4 (2006).
26 Jane Gillette, "Can Gardens Mean?", *Landscape Journal*, 24 (2005), p.95.

120 History "invented" for site today

enthralling, but it can never be the same as responding to the garden *in situ*, not least because (to say this once again) there is no definite route around it and we must factor our impressions into a coherent whole *outside the garden*, which is precisely what a book can do.

There are various clues within the site, including many inscriptions, some straightforward and more that are (as befits such injunctions) gnomic, such as "LORENTZ TRANSFORMATION RELATING LENGTHS IN DIFFERENT REFERENCES FRAMES" or "MASS EQUALS ENERGY" on the roof of the greenhouse; equations "$Xn+1=BXn(1-Xn$"; Ambigrams, or words that can be read upside-down; Baudelaire's lines on "Correspondences" ("La nature est un temple...."), the lines of which at least urge us to try and interpret this "nature" – where confused words ("Confuses paroles"), a forest of symbols ("des forêts de symbols") and perfumes, colours and sounds ("parfums, les couleurs, et les sons") assail us; eight red poles face north; grass mounds with sharp, clean modern edges and paths that recall earlier *Schneckenberge* or snail mounts; water bodies shaped in half moons and curlicues that curl and twist below the mounds; globes depicting various constellations; models of atoms; a fractal terrace, its multi-coloured squares breaking up "as they approach nature", or the terrace of converging green and white squares that vanish into an apparently rotating black hole.

But two elements in particular are both clear and less puzzling. A series of wonderful gates take the form of "soliton waveforms" that "travel through each other and keep their identity, that is, *a memory of the past*" (my italics), as waves of energy travel through the metal twists and turns of the ironwork. That solitons were theorized by a Scotsman also localizes them here in the Lowlands, this acknowledgement of that remembered past is potent. The other event is the bright white "staircase" or descending terrace of slabs known as the Universe Cascade, which also dramatizes the past, but now of deep time (Figure 6.9). The steps of this cascade are scattered with inscribed equations and decorated with strange forms that announce at every step different moments of cosmic history, as we ascend from the worlds of quarks and fogs, then into plasma, photons and galactic clouds, and then into something a touch more graspable – steps that measure billions and millions of years, the coming of the solar system and the earth and its planets, the Cambrian explosion, animals, sex, mass extinctions and eventually after 12.999948 billion years "consciousness", civilization, and ecology threatened by modern economics. If we want historical ground, this is clearly IT.

The book offers one clear "clue in the Garden – Self-Organizing Harmonies" (p.240). In the end, as gardens are first and foremost, if not finally, a visual art, it is the colours and shapes that we enjoy, and the enjoyment of its forms that we are presented with; that these are often coded with metaphors will dawn on us slowly (another clue perhaps that Jencks' book offers: p.33). But it is we who self-organize its offered harmonies, as they haunt us on site and afterwards.

Fifty or so miles to the east of the Garden of Cosmic Speculation is another garden, created by Ian Hamilton Finlay and his wife at Little Sparta (as it is now

FIGURE 6.9 The Garden of Cosmic Speculation, Portrack House, near Dumfries in South West Scotland. The Universe Cascade. (Courtesy of Charles Jencks).

called).[27] This too, though radically different from that created by Jencks, established another wonderful garden where, if there were some history to the place (family connections or agricultural history) this was surpassed; this was originally a small croft, with a solitary tree set within an expanse of moorland. What was projected and slowly established over the years was a place responsive to Finlay's own understanding of his place in political and garden history. Little Sparta, originally named Stony Path, became a place where a wealth of historical references was stored and exploited. Finlay was always a poet ("Makar" in Scots) as well as a garden-maker, and, like Touchstone, what poetry he choose to feign was also true.

The historical ground constructed at Little Sparta consisted in inventing fresh perspectives on garden–making, based notably on Finlay's famous "Unconnected Sentences of Gardening", one of which remarks that gardens, usually thought of as retreats, were more surely "attacks". Thus everywhere on the site visitors would confront injunctions, direct or implied, to (re)consider what a garden was in both its own gardenist terms and in the larger landscape beyond (not the actual Lowlands, but the philosophical and imaginative land elsewhere in space and time).

27 I have written a book on the garden art of Finlay, and of course focused much on this particular garden: *Nature Over Again* (London: Reaktion Books, 2008). What is discussed here is briefer and focused wholly on the issue of historical ground that was not touched upon in my earlier book. See also Yves Abrioux, *Ian Hamilton Finlay: A Visual Primer* (London: Reaktion, 1985) and Jessie Sheeler, *Little Sparta: the Garden of Ian Hamilton Finlay* (London: Frances Lincoln, 2003).

There are machine guns (at the very beginning of the driveway up to the garden), bronze-coloured fibreglass tortoises with PANZER LEADER engraved on their shells in the front garden, a bird table in the form of aircraft carrier (where the birds swoop down to pluck the crumbs), a temple dedicated to Apollo that celebrates the Muses and his Music, but also the "MISSILES" that he launched ("Apollo" being a term also applied to the rocket programme); a golden but decapitated head of Apollo will be discovered in the groves with APOLLON TERRORISTE written on its forehead, and Apollo (again) chases Daphne through the groves (Figure 6.10). Finlay here and elsewhere plays with his love for boats and ships, flowers, and their capacity for loss and destruction: the elaborate row of brick plinths at the edge of the moorland at Little Sparta that commemorate naval ships whose names are

FIGURE 6.10 Little Sparta, Dunsyre near Edinburgh, Scotland. Ian Hamilton Finlay, steel cut-out figures after Bernini's Apollo and Daphne (Photograph Emily T. Cooperman).

History "invented" for site today **123**

'camouflaged' in the names of flowers, or in his design elsewhere, for Portland Bill in Dorset, that celebrated the cruisers torpedoed during WWII, with a quotation from Virgil about souls on the River Styx unable to cross to the underworld, this last aptly sited on true historical ground. Against these intimations of war and revolution are poised other gestures: not only to flowers, but to the painter Claude Lorrain, injunctions to recognize Arcadia in this particular Scottish landscape (admittedly inscribed on a broken column), and the delight in the workaday world of gardening (tools, a wheelbarrow, a greenhouse).

Now none of this is immediately historical, though everything here implies some historical moment, either local to Scotland or to a larger international scene; some references are light and gently ironic, others darker and bleaker: classical quotations and neo-classical references, the French Revolution (guillotines, quotations from the Jacobite Saint Just), the lettering on Scottish fishing boats that signal their home port, pastoralism, German Romanticism, neo-Platonism. The range of reference and the scope of the garden are wide, but none unfocused.

All these references come from history, selected to be sure and manipulated by Finlay to serve his own imaginative ends, and they all require some careful and often knowledgeable elucidation ("Working out … Finlay's brief excerptions [of others' writing] … is not the work of an idle moment"[28]). But the site of Little Sparta – itself a name that conjures the ancient rivalry of Athens to its enemy/rival Sparta and the local appellation of Edinburgh as the Athens of the north – is rich in historical meanings. These are localized here – like Shakespeare's Theseus, they are given "a local habitation and a name", and thereby the various strands of history find a fresh vantage point from which to interrogate or admonish the modern world. It has been a theme of many discussions of historical grounds to acknowledge, also, a future: an inscribed group of stone blocks from 1983 at Little Sparta reads THE PRESENT ORDER IS THE DISORDER OF THE FUTURE.[29]

If Little Sparta creates a new garden *ex nihilo* and is the most detailed and instructive piece of garden art by Finlay, he has nevertheless intervened, less fully, on various other sites, where the location guided what he proposed. Finlay himself observed that his "particular talent is for making use of whatever possibility is there".[30] He did this in what turned out to be an aborted and frustrated installation

---

28 Quoted from Harry Gilonis's unpublished remarks on Finlay at a recent Tate Gallery exhibition. Neither he nor I would say that everything in Finlay needs "decoding", though some historical allusions and gestures surely do.

29 These stones are cracked and slightly broken, and lie on the ground, perhaps ready to be used for a future building; the words are those of the Jacobin, Louis-Antoine Saint-Just, guillotined in 1794 at the age of 27. So the modern invocation of this remark suggests both a historical pessimism and an optimistic future.

30 In an interview with Paul Crowther, cited in *Nature Over Again,* p.171. Other Finlay sites that attend to their locality are discussed in my book, and these include installations in places like the Celle Sculpture Park near Pistoia, Italy, the Kröller-Müller Museum in The Netherlands, the Serpentine Gallery in Hyde Park, and the botanical gardens at the University of Durham, UK, within the sound of the cathedral bells. The instances here are discussed and illustrated in my book on Finlay.

124 History "invented" for site today

(killed by the animosity of critics who misread his work): this was a proposal for a *bosquet* for the Hôtel des Menus Plaisirs at Versailles, contributed as part of the celebrations to mark the bicentenary of the French Revolution on the site where the Estates General had debated the Declaration of the Rights of Man and the Citizen (Figure 6.11). The grove of poplars (a pun on the French *peuple*, populace) and cherry trees, a Genette-like reference to an incidence in Rousseau's *Confessions*, would have been interspersed with huge blocks of stone on which was inscribed a quotation from the historian Michelet: NOUS VOULIONS GRAVER NOTRE LOI SUR LA PIERRE DU DROIT ETERNEL SUR LE ROC QUI PORTE LE MONDE L'INVARIABLE JUSTICE ET L'INDESTRUCTIBLE EQUITE (We would wish to engrave out law on the stone of eternal right on the rock that brings the world invariable justice and indestructible equity). Differently, and successfully, for St George's, Brandon Hill in Bristol, a redundant church now used for concerts, some of the usual Finlay elements are there – benches, inscriptions, a post: they feature quotations from Virgil on songs, a line from Ovid on the passage of air into a reed, then into the air and thence into music, and translations of letters by Janacek. In the grounds of a physics research institute, the Max Planck in Stuttgart, he plays with the Latin for "wave": this is a theme he has

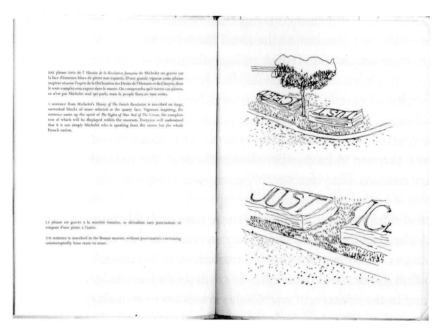

FIGURE 6.11 Ian Hamilton Finlay, with Alexandre Chemetoff, Sue Finlay and Nicholas Sloan, an opening of "Le Jardin révolutionnaire", Hôtel des Menus Plaisirs, Versailles, 1988. (Annenberg Rare Book & Manuscript Library, University of Pennsylvania Libraries).

History "invented" for site today **125**

explored in other places and contexts, but here – as the Latin word unveils itself in a series of letters, corrected with the printer's correction mark of a wavy line to read, eventually, VNDA – he illustrates a central item in physics.[31] In the Stockwood Park at Luton, on a former meadowland adjacent to, and separated by a ha-ha from, a former garden, are a flock of "sheep": scattered blocks of stone, inscribed with a remark that records how Pythagoreans thought men were flocks in the property of gods who would not let them leave the fold (the stones are, therefore, aptly immovable). Yet in each case, Finlay has used a particular site to enlarge how he sees local possibilities and to gesture outwards to a much larger history of thought and action.

A further cluster of new landscapes, where none had existed before and where no strong history, if any, animated the site, can suggest the potential and the challenge of true invention. Kathryn Gustafson's Jardins de l'Imaginaire are what its name implies: imaginary fragments, as Udo Weilacher says, of garden history.[32] A small village in Perigord established four gardens in the 1990s, three of which were "classical", in addition to Gustafson's, which she won in a competition that asked for a garden that linked Italian gardens, French baroque, Japanese gardens and, given the topography, "English" naturalism. Hers took a variety of hints from the terraces of local agriculture and then from a repertoire of garden fountains and theatres, rose gardens, greenhouses, and pools and chains of water; in fact, all her motifs could be said to be "classical"; but were presented in ways that, by being unexpected in format or location, would strike visitors as invented, while at the same time perhaps reminding them of their original inspiration in garden histories.

The garden theatre is a familiar item in many early, usually southern gardens[33]: but the seats here in the Jardins de l'Imaginaire are somewhat scattered, more intimate, and not continuous as in an ancient Greek theatre; both they, and the steps down the "auditorium", are in black painted steel. Below and distantly, but to the side of where a theatre's platform would be, is what appears to be the surface of a circular lake. This trompe-l'oeil, another Renaissance reference, is actually the glass roof of the circular greenhouse, seen from above; this was designed by Ian Ritchie and its walls constructed of gabions. The forest of jetting fountains (*Forêt des jets*) matches the surrounding woodland through which paths navigate, and is set in a variegated brick and stone garden, cut through with a narrow channel. Elsewhere, a narrow water table – think perhaps of Vaux le Vicomte or Courances, but here raised above ground like an aqueduct – contrasts its strict formality and narrow

31 Cf. the understandings and realizations of wave in the Garden of Cosmic Speculation (above).

32 *In Gardens*, pp.100–7, quoting p.100. See also Hervé Brunon and Monique Mosser, *Le Jardin contemporain: Renouveau, expérieneces et enjeux* (Paris: nouvelles editions SCALA, 2011), pp.62–4. See also Chapter Seven below, note 29.

33 See chapter 5 on "Garden and Theatre" in *Garden and Grove: The Italian Renaissance Garden in the English Imagination: 1600–1750*, (London, 1986; new paperback edition, University of Pennsylvania Press, 1996), and "Garden as Theatre", chapter 9 in *A World of Gardens* (London: Reaktion Books, 2012).

126 History "invented" for site today

length with the otherwise "natural" landscaping above it. The garden implies narratives (references to Ariadne, wind games and bells in the trees), and Weilacher seems to accept this move ("telling stories from all epochs of garden culture"). There is a water staircase, a rose garden – a steel pergola that "looks like a magic carpet of flowers", a sacred wood (*un bois sacré*) and miniature fountains to represent four great rivers of the world in Egypt, Mesopotamia, India and the United States. Like almost all garden narratives, this one offers nothing continuous, having no defined route, despite following Ariadne's thread through the woods from the village, or out again; but its tales, its *imaginary*, come in fragments, even for the "well-versed" visitor, to whom Weilacher appeals. That it clearly "feigns", in the manner of Touchstone's aphorism, is wonderfully apparent: whether it is the "truest poetry" is less sure.

Three gardens in Provence were made in spaces where none had existed before, in a farmland, among olive groves, or besides a mansion. At least two obviously respond to a general sense of locality: Provence itself, and a northerner's nostalgia for the "warm south" ("Goethe's Law"[34]), to its geology (one site has abundant water), local farming, and local culture; agricultural infrastructure in one case, indigenous buildings in another. Yet in all cases – though they are indeed a very varied trio – we are met with places that privilege the imaginary over any acknowledgement of a particular place and history.[35]

Near the town of Uzès, the Jardin de la Noria took its name from the mechanism by which water is drawn from below ground in wooden or leathern buckets and distributed in channels through the surrounding area; the *noria* is an ancient Arabic device, illustrated in old documents, and some still survive in southern Europe and north Africa. This one is mounted on a stone platform (Figure 6.12) and works by moving a horizontal pole, manipulated by a donkey or a person, that pulls the water up and drops it into the channel to flow off the platform and into the orchard. This whole property is an ancient Provencal farmhouse or *mas*, a property that comprises a *potager*, a rosary, a prairie of fruit trees, a grove of fir trees and a contemporary swimming pool, so the need for water supply makes sense. But the surroundings of the noria are a more studied confection of Mediterranean ideas, and its designers are versed in that garden culture.[36] A narrow basin recalls the long pool in the Generalife in Granada; *kiosques* add another slightly Turkish tonality. Terracotta pots, a typical feature, are unusual in both shape and decoration, and like the benches (with inward turning

---

34 Patrick Leigh Fermor, *A Time of Gifts* (New York: New York Review Books, 2005), p. 222, commenting on the yearning of "All dwellers in the Teutonic north" for the warm Mediterranean.

35 I have discussed these three gardens in more detail, and with an emphasis on how they reveal the meanings (which I avoid here) in my chapter on "Meaning" in A *Cultural History of Gardens*, ed. Michael Leslie and John Dixon Hunt, vol.6 (London: Bloomsbury, 2013).

36 Its designers are Eric Ossart and Arnaud Maurières, authors of the book, *Jardiniers de Paradis* (Paris: Editions du Chêne, 2000).

History "invented" for site today 127

FIGURE 6.12 Le Jardin de la Noria, near Uzès, Provence, France. The ancient noria is raised on a plinth at the rear of the terrace, with a spout for the water to pour into the channel that disappears into the orchard at the left. (Photo: Emily T. Cooperman).

feet) and seats (in the form of a simple zigzag in warm, painted rust-red concrete), are emphatically modern. While the property as a whole accepts the name that derives from the area immediately around the *noria*, this is still a studied and contrived invocation of a culture that is not here, either locally or maybe not even historically.

The same designers, Ossart and Maurières, also designed Le Jardin de l'Alchimiste, near the town of Eygalières (Figure 6.13). Its name makes clear, as the labelling and identification of the various sections of the garden also do, that this draws upon traditions of alchemy. The garden begins with a labyrinth that meanders in a form that spells out the word *Berechit* (the first word of the Hebrew bible signifying origin or beginning); that leads to the "Garden of Magical Plants" arranged in square beds, and finally to a third segment where larger squares are dedicated to red, white and black gardens; these propose a "sens spirituel" and are derived from ancient kabbalistic lore. It is not a garden that you can miss, even if the kabbala and the alchemical significances escape you: the elaborate layout, especially the elegant channels of water, that hint perhaps of Islamic forms, and the overall colours and perfumes within a fairly small space, all make a strong impression. People clearly enjoy it, and it suggests that this invented garden, which

128 History "invented" for site today

FIGURE 6.13 Le Jardin de l'Alchimiste, Provence, France.

has no need to be here or indeed in Provence, can for some visitors elicit a true sense of its poetry.

Further east in Provence is the third garden, Fleur de l'Air, designed by Ian Hamilton Finlay.[37] Unlike the other two gardens, this is not open to the public, and it expresses, through Finlay's gardenist imagination, the private owner's strong sense and love of Provence (Figure 6.14). The site is large, and established on a hillside,

---

37 Finlay's Wild Hawthorne Press published a book on this garden, *Fleur de l'Air: A Garden in Provence* (2004), with photographs by Volkmar Herre, commentaries by Harry Gilonis and an essay by myself. For a more extended essay on the garden's rich allusions and how this ground has found for itself a new history, see Gilonis's essay, "Where time becomes space – Ian Hamilton Finlay's garden in Provence", *Word & Image,* 21/4 (2005), pp.308–22.

History "invented" for site today 129

FIGURE 6.14 Ian Hamilton Finlay, stones carved with words of the French historian Michelet, Fleur de l'Air, Provence, France. (Photo: Emily T. Cooperman).

where stone terraces descend through the olive groves to its wilder area, where wild boar roam and a dual bust of Jean-Jacques Rousseau, perhaps alluding to his reveries of a solitary walker, gazes at himself and at the anagrams of his name inscribed on the plinths. Throughout the landscape are typical and familiar moves – blocks of inscribed stone, urns, seats, pools, a *tempietto* and other tree plaques dedicated to the Provencal dialogue between light with shade, allusions to the songs of Eurydice heard in the woods and mountains, but echoing Pope's "Ode for Musick". But also our attention is drawn to both the place itself, the olives groves, the nearby Mediterranean, lavender and rosemary, an old *cabane,* and to a world of poets – to Petrarch, whose gardens in Provence were dedicated to Bacchus and to Apollo and the Muses (and busts of these latter are grouped in a circle at the entrance to the property), to Goethe quoted for his love of the south, myrtles and

130 History "invented" for site today

citrus trees. A bronze oar wrapped as with netting, inscribed simply with HOM.OD.XI., alludes gnomically to the *Odyssey* and its hero's wanderings and an exchange in Book XI between seafarers and those on land who know not the sea.[38] It is a place that speaks almost literally to the visitor by virtue of the device of *prosopopoeia*, by which a poet imagines being addressed by something in the landscape. That many of the utterances can be gnomic or unfamiliar allows scope for unpacking the allusions, honours its owner who has worked with Finlay to establish the garden, and at the same time creates a unique historical ground that makes sense of this Provencal location and yet establishes it in a wider world of ideas.

There is, I suspect, always a touch of humour if not outright irony in all of these invented gardens. The rubbing-post where the itchy wild boar scratches itself and rolls in a mudbath, usefully provided nearby, is wholly apt for this district roamed by actual wild boars, and its elegant bronze pole is inscribed with a line used by Plautus who addresses – the boar, the visitor, us? – with AGE QUOD AGIS (what are you doing?). It may be that some historical ground, established where nothing apparently existed of it earlier or where a poet has seized the unexpected, is likely to be ironic. Though some people can be disturbed by irony (that speaks one thing and means another, a garden that is itself but also speaks of elsewhere), it can be both fun in itself and draw oblique attention to the play of meanings on a site; of which there are many in any Finlay garden. The Jardin Atlantique, for example, is playful and witty, and it touches ironically on those who either know they have no chance to reach the Atlantic coast or who realize that the garden is but a "play" or "*jeu*". The COLAS gardens cherish their amusing dialogue with past gardens, and there is a strongly ironic push against a merely pastoral or "naturalistic" attitude towards gardens. When Abalos & Herreros make an existing incinerator into "a new waste-to-energy generator"[39] in Barcelona there is, probably unintentionally, a witty juxtaposition of such an improbable item with a waterfront beach and parkland. Certain landscapes are often saying to be "rolling" and pastoral, gently spreading their inland waves across the territory: but Gustafson's Shell Petroleum HQ outside Paris invoke rolling berms and hilly lawns both to hide an underground parking garage and to mitigate the modernist steel and glass building. Tall, steel lamp shafts in a pool look like "giant drill bits", and they celebrate Shell's "on-going exploration of natural resources".[40] All good satire has the tendency to celebrate what it protests, merely by the wit and elegance of the protest itself.

Often a humourist, Martha Schwartz's early decision to fill a pool at an early (now defunct) shopping centre in Atlanta with gold frogs played with both the bathos of cheap garden centre décor and the golden lure of a shopping centre

---

38 In particular, for some elucidation of these intricate paratextual references, see Gilonis, *Fleur de L'Air*, note on Plate 63.

39 *Groundswell*, pp.144–7.

40 Ibid, pp.90–4.

(Figure 6.15).[41] Many people flock to garden centres to buy both plants and often gardens ornaments for their homes; landscape architects can stick their noses in the air over such *déclassé* items, but when it seemed apt for a temporary installation in Germany, Martha Schwartz bought 51 garden ornaments from garden-store chains: these were then mounted, as in any museum, on white boxes. This cabinet of curious pigs, flamingos, windmills, dwarves, plastic classical sculptures, sheep, glass balls, wells, and lamps held aloft by woolly dogs or black jockeys characterized a "collective landscape", familiar and ubiquitous that "seemed to reflect who we are and how we would be seen".[42]

Her work here and elsewhere is often about the idea of the garden and how it "seemed" to show us as we were: what it might have been and what – in often

FIGURE 6.15 Martha Schwartz, frogs in a pool at a redundant shopping centre, Atlanta, Georgia.

41 *The Vanguard Landscapes and Gardens of Martha Schwartz*, p.158 and for the next, p.104. The frogs at Atlanta are perhaps a further allusion to the frogs gathered around the fountain of Latona in Versailles, with its reference there to political events in the Fronde.
42 Ibid, pp.192–7. Cf. how the owners of Villa d'Este or Villa Lante or Vaux le Vicomte reflected who they were and how they wished to be seen

132 History "invented" for site today

changed circumstances, economic and social – it now needed to be. Why did it have to be "nature" (when many garden owners have arguably never seen the "real thing", or when there was never any "real nature' left anyway)? Why did we flatter ourselves with evocations of an elitism that we couldn't afford? Or comfort ourselves with the nostalgia of lost retreats? Her humour is often extremely pointed: when lack of funds prevented her using real royal palms trees, she devised sixteen canopies of vinyl-coated steel to recall the displaced Everglade trees that once flourished where the Broward County Civic Arena now stands in Fort Lauderdale, Florida.[43] The irony of that invention is far more pointed and poignant than any planting of actual palms. But professional landscape architects are not prone or eager to be ironic; that is left, often, to designers who work in garden festivals or for private patrons where the opportunity for some surrealist plays is welcomed.[44]

Avant gardeners

So we get to what Tim Richardson, in a wonderful phrase, has termed "avant gardeners". As Touchstone remarked, with irony yet with absolute conviction, the "truest poetry is [or may be] the most feigning". It is also like Baudolino's stories that seem, even if outright lies, convincing to the extent that a real historian to whom he tells his tales is seduced, or maybe hoodwinked, by their plausibility. We might seek analogies to this search for "true poetry" in the built work of those designers whom Tim Richardson, in his book on *Avant Gardeners,* calls "Conceptualists".[45] What these apparently have in common are "the harnessing of an idea, or set of related ideas, as the starting point for work that was characterized by the use of colour, artificial materials and witty commentary on a site's history and culture".[46] This is opposed to "the functionalist imperatives of Modernism … the decorative or romantic tradition of the 19th century … and the avowedly naturalist stance…".This is, therefore, a somewhat mixed grouping of designers; yet beyond the contrived rhetorical rivalry proposed by Richardson lurks an interesting issue about how or when to handle history in landscape architecture.

The conceptualist commentary on a site's history is taken up specifically in his essay on "History" (pp.97–104). Modernists, we are told, display an "ignorance of history [that is] a hallmark of mediocrity in the avant-garde of any medium"; and while Richardson is right to bypass postmodernism's pandering to "a catalogue of

43 Ibid, pp.104–7; even the title of this project is ironic – "ghosts of the everglades light the way".
44 For examples, look at those explored by Weilacher in *In Gardens*, at Chandigarh or at the Tarot Garden in Italy (pp.169–81). And see Chapter Seven for more discussion of historical ground in garden festivals.
45 See also below in Chapter Seven for a discussion of conceptualism in garden festivals.
46 *Avant Gardeners* (London:Thames & Hudson. 2008), p.9; it is, though, a phrase that could apply to many much earlier gardens. Further references to this intriguing book will be in the text.

History "invented" for site today **133**

reusable features" from the past, these are unsubtle generalizations. Furthermore, while he equates history with meaning, or with "landscape as metaphor", neither of these need be the substance of historical ground. These remarks derive in part from a somewhat skewed analysis that he borrows from Mario Terzic: opposing an anti-*historical* approach ("based on prejudice and ignorance") with an anti-*historicist* one ("founded on knowledge and a belief in the power of newness in art"). Surely the sense of a *historical* past must also be based, not only on a firm knowledge of that past, but also on grasping the *difference* between the past and the present; this empowers newness in art because it registers that difference; this is the true usefulness of historicism.[47] For when we can recognize that difference, the past can be seen to have been enmeshed in a context with spatial and temporal reference points that established its specific habit of mind: "a web of relations that define it as unique and, at the same time, typify it ... a product of its own unique process of development". That is the proper historicist position: not aping the past, but observing historical difference enough to see how a new art might be formed (so here I agree with Richardson). This new art responds to its own contemporary "web of relations".

One of the issues with avant-garde conceptualists that Richardson discusses is whether they can make a new place, even if it is temporary (as in designs for garden festivals, which are taken up in the following chapter), rather than simply a spectacle or what has been called a "non-place". One of the appeals of all good designs, whether permanent or temporary, is their "polyphony" (we might also call it a palimpsest), "in which the virtually infinite interlacing of destinies, actions, thoughts and reminiscences would rest on a bass line that chimed the hours of the terrestrial day, and marked the position that used to be (and could still be) occupied there by an ancient ritual".[48] The musical analogy – the bass line of a melody, and the play of variations – is also invoked by Jean Starobinski and also by Schiffman: invoking Baudelaire (also Joyce), he suggests how modernity was a "willed coexistence of two different worlds", where the bass line of today allows or sustains the play of "ritual", or "thoughts and reminiscences". This modernity, where today accommodates yesterday's recollections, is contrasted with what Marc Augé calls a supermodernity: a "realm of non-places", *without reference* to "an event (which has taken place), a myth (said to have taken place) or a history". This transforms history into a mere "element of spectacle", as the supermodernist only "makes the old [history] into a specific spectacle, as it does with all exoticism and all local particularity". They are simply "quotations" of the old. But for a true modernity, we look to the "interweaving of old and new".

This strenuous, non-spectacular understanding of place (even though designs may still be striking and in that sense spectacular) is the basis of an invented

---

47 I am indebted here to a long and difficult discussion by Zachary Sayre Schiffman, *The Birth of the Past* (2011), quoting (pp. 12 and 3).

48 I borrow these remarks from Marc Augé, *Non-places: Introduction to an anthropology of supermodernity* (London: Verso, 1995); it is he who cites Starobinski.

134 History "invented" for site today

historical ground that runs through some, but not all, of Richardson's short essays or designers' statements that he cites. But they do not all make the best of this polyphony. He is right to inveigh against Gross.Max's "office credo – 'to reveal the different layers of the landscape'" (the firm prefers "striptease" rather than palimpsest), which does not, says Richardson, result in "an extensive historical survey of the site". Their new park at Potters Field, for example (pp.116–17), may gesture to its history with a strip of Deftware patterns cutting through the customary grass as "a reference to the local 17th-century porcelain trade" of Potters Field; its planting by the Dutch designer and plantsman Piet Oudolf is also presumably meant to underline this Dutch connection.

Gustafson/Porter, already explored in Chapter Five, are, along with Martha Schwartz, to whose work Richardson had already devoted an earlier book, constitute his favourite examples. Of the former's work, he selects their Diana Memorial in Hyde Park, and a former gasworks site in Amsterdam. These are real and usable places that properly connect the old with the new and even the future. The site in Amsterdam, preserving vestiges of some gasometers, re-invents a by-now familiar mode of reminding users of an industrial past that in many responses are clapped out or outmoded. Whether this is *avant-garde* is moot, but the creation of a lake (and adjacent canals in the vicinity) speak of Amsterdam, and as the lake can be drained for events, watched by an audience on the grass field that slopes down to it, the site has a new and versatile existence. It is not clear, again, how Gustafson/Porter's Diana Memorial in Hyde Park is avant-garde; but it makes a new place in the park that does something different, that will attract visitors as long as the memory of the Princess of Wales remains: Porter argues that "In five or ten years, it will look [with its glade of fully grown *Cladastris kentukea*] like it has always been there", which is a true mark of invented historical ground. The generous sculpted slope with the variety of engineered water effects ("from bubbling cauldron to swooshing smoothness" [Richardson's description]) may well mirror Diana's character.[49] But it is the firm's iconic idiom and invocation of basic garden elements – sculptured forms, terraces, pools and the generosity of open space that mark much of their work – rather than its specific appeal to history that is telling; families and children play there happily and the relaxation is palpable. In that sense, the Garden of Forgiveness in Lebanon is unusual with its overt recognition and celebration of the spirit of historical ground; while they tend to rely on whatever history or myth or event offers, they do not force it at either Amsterdam or London, and they attend specifically to present affects.

Beyond the cluster of so-called conceptualists identified and discussed by Richardson, we can find other examples of a feigned history. Certainly, invention of a total historical *ground* is rare – after all, the Jardin Atlantique is unusual in constructing its own ground or platform over the Montparnasse station and in invoking, less the station below, than the distant destination of the Atlantic coast.

49 *Avant Gardeners*, pp.128–9 (for Amsterdam) and p.124 (for Diana's Fountain).

More often, it is that a designer takes over a site and uses its ground or its materials as the basis for something new – this applies to the now innumerable ways in which derelict landscapes become the foundation of new work. Occasionally, as with Duisburg or the High Line, the infrastructure is left as the groundwork for the new and reveals that earlier culture. More infrequently, existing materials provide the resources for the new device.

The courtyard of pine cones created by WEST 8 for a monastery in Padua in 2003 is at once simple and inventive – layering a whole courtyard with pine trees from the tree that shades it. Whether or not the descent of the many, many pine cones onto the ground is a miracle, as is locally believed, the combination of the scent of the resin, their slightly reddish colouring, along with its sly attention to the future – for the seeds drop out of the cones and sprout through the strange and wonderful carpet – make a fresh "miracle" of the groundcover; a perforated steel walkway allows visitors to see the massed pine cones beneath them.[50]

Similarly, where there is nothing but an overgrown ravine, discovered at the end of a narrow path through bamboo groves – "Percorso fra I Bambù" – Paolo Bürgi has made a small balcony overlooking the ravine: with a seat for one, or maybe two persons (Figure 6.16); in this reclusive and green spot ("Annihilating all that's

FIGURE 6.16 Paolo Bürgi, private garden, Padua, Italy. The end of the Percorso fra I Bambù, 1999. (Photo courtesy of the designer).

50 *Mosaics,* WEST 8, pp.154–7.

136 History "invented" for site today

made, To a green thought in a green shade") we contemplate where we are (and are allowed time to know ourselves as well). Bürgi did it again, with a larger terrace and with benches in each side, overlooking an alluvial landscape, run to seed and "visually unattractive" (as Bürgi explained[51]); so this became another spot for contemplation, and one that ensures that this spot had a meaning that is probably renewed every time it is visited by its owners or their guests. Maybe in a country like Switzerland, so overwhelmed by its territory and the resources of its countryside and mountains, a landscape architect's response has inevitably to allow the locality its prominent share, whether unattractive or compelling. Whether it be large and sublime, as at Cardada, or small and intimate on the walk through the bamboos or out onto the terrace, the place itself furnishes the design and the affecting experience.

Bürgi loves to exploit the materials of the ground where he works, especially trees. He might make a spiral enclosure of lofty specimens near a factory, or, at a rather uncared-for and unattractive psychiatric hospital at Mendrisio, in the Ticino, Switzerland, he established a series of arboreal "follies" on a wandering route through the park (Figure 6.17). People are entertained by both the slow growth –

FIGURE 6.17 Paolo Bürgi, Tree "follies" – perspective, and false perspective – at the Organizzazione Sociopsichiatria Cantonale, Mendrisio, Ticino, Switzerland, 1986–89. (Photography courtesy of the designer).

51 Paolo Bürgi, *Paesaggi-Passaggi*, p.117. The terrace is discussed and illustrated on the subsequent pages, as are the following projects. The tree "follies" are discussed by Bürgi in *Topos /European Landscape Magazine,* 42 (2003), pp.37–47, and by Michael Rohde and Rainer Schomann, *Historic Gardens Today* (Leipzig, Germany: Edition Leipzig, 2003), pp.66–71.

some trees will take three hundred years to grow into their projected form, a tree house is open to the sky (for the moment), but some follies create immediate effects, such as *trompe l'oeil* perspectives looking different ways down lines of *Cupressus sempervirens*, or hornbeams made into a twisted and surrealist plant sculpture that will eventually form a tall, thick hedge.

Bürgi's work is poetic[52] – in that the designs are most feigned, but true to the local materials he calls upon. They may take a while for visitors to appreciate them; though no conceptualist, he believes that a place is sustained by a distinct and enlivening idea, and that – by perhaps accepting metaphorical meanings – it may be offered to those users/visitors who may respond to that poetry: "I believe that in order to communicate with the users of a site, you must choose a few important elements, and make people feel their presence".

52 *Paolo Bürgi: Landscape Architect,* op. cit., p.95. That one of his favourite words is "beautiful", an Englishing of "che bello" in Italian, also suggests his appeal to the poetic.

7

LAND ART, GARDEN FESTIVALS AND HISTORICAL GROUND

It could be asked how and in what way is land art related to these discussions of historical ground[1]; on the face of it, land art seems to have nothing to do with landscape architecture. But then, the notion that much land art was focused upon doing something to reveal the character and significance of a particular site and its materials connects with my sense of history's role in contemporary landscape design. So it is a topic that, finally, I need to address – first by asking to what extent land art is, or can coincide with, landscape architecture, and if so how does it address the history of a site; and then by extending the topic to look at non-permanent events, like garden festivals. For in these festivals, something akin to land art, designers find a temporary site that may address historical events or ideas not usually associated with it. Many landscape architects are now engaging in these festivals or garden shows (the list of exhibitors at Métis garden festival in Canada makes this very clear), so that the role of an invented history seems to have gained a new currency.

When a group of landscape architects were asked during the late 1990s about how their work related to land art, most were at best noncommittal, others somewhat negative.[2] None of them, however, actually addressed what seems to be the essential difference between these related, but ultimately distinct, activities: put in its basic terms, landscape architects design places to be used, to be lived in; they

---

1   It was John Beardsley, after a lecture on this theme at Dumbarton Oaks, who posed that question to me: very apt, since he himself has written much and intelligently about land art and its modernist appeal.
2   I depend largely upon the book of these interviews published by Udo Weilacher in *Between Landscape Architecture and Land Art* (Berlin: Birkhäuser, 1999), for which I wrote a short introduction; also *Land and Environmental Art*, ed. Jeffrey Kastner, with survey by Brian Wallis (London: Phaidon, 1988), and Gilles A. Tiberghien, *Nature, Art, Paysage* (Arles, France: Actes Sud, 2001).

are social places, even if they are private; occasionally they may include a distant scene that is to be viewed rather than entered or lived in – "borrowed scenery" in Chinese terms, "calling in the country" in Pope's words, or having "picturesque" experiences. "Using" and "living in" a place may also be a stretch if we think of the new vogue for vertical gardens, like the Quai Branly Museum in Paris, or Ken Smith's Atrium Garden, New York. But mostly landscape architects design places for inhabitation.[3]

Land art does not do that. We can visit, and even walk down into, "Double Negative" by Michael Heizer in the Nevada desert near Overton; but we do not inhabit it (Figure 7.1). Robert Smithson's "Spiral Jetty" can be walked upon, we can wander its spirals as we gaze at the crystals in the water of the Great Salt Lake in Utah, but we do not dwell there. Into Walter de Maria's "Lightning Field" (near Quemado, New Mexico) we certainly do not enter, except to examine the poles when thunders storms are not threatening: otherwise we watch the lightning from a safe distance as it strikes the poles, performed as a spectacle for us in a theatre of weather. And in many other cases, though we may enter into a given space, descend into Mary Miss's underground hole from "Perimeters/Pavilions/Decoys" of 1977–78, or crouch in Nancy Holt's "Sun Tunnels" on the Great Basin Desert in Utah (1973–78)[4], we do not "dwell" there (neither in its commonsensical, nor in

FIGURE 7.1 Michael Heizer, Double Negative, Nevada Desert, near Overton, NV.

---

3 For Branley, see Evelyn Lee, "Patrick Blanc's Vertical Gardens", *inhabitat* (29 January 2011); *Ken Smith: Landcsape Architect* (New York: Monacelli Press, 2009), pp.72–87.
4 Illustrated in *Land and Environmental Art*, p.105 and in Gilles A. Tiberghien, *Land Art* (Paris: Editions Carré, 1993), pp.147–9.

140 Land art and garden festivals

Heidegger's more special, meaning). Robert Smithson makes clear that connections between sites of dwelling and his own form of land art are at best problematic when he asks "Could one say that art degenerates as it approached gardening?"[5]

Yet many sites of land art are themselves striking, and often they reveal the site where they are located – where lightning strikes (literally), where the *mesa* is carved in deep trenches to help us see its edge condition, where trees trunks are woven horizontally in a forest, or a dry-stone wall winds between trees like a snake or a slalom skier.[6] They engage with natural materials even if they do not depict it (a formulation proposed by John Beardsley[7]), and they can change and restructure space, which we then see anew. Many also rely essentially upon time and weather – when the lightning strikes, when tree trunks decay or ice sculptures melt, when a pattern of interlaced leaves floating in a stream lose themselves in the water, when "Spiral Jetty" is submerged in the rising lake, or even when time crumbles the sharp edges of "Double Negative". And geology and seasons also provide opportunities, when holes are drilled into the earth, or when Herman Prigann's "Gelbe Rampe" ("Yellow Ramp") is surrounded with concrete slabs from adjacent mining access roads and crowns its summit with an archaic calendar structure that marks the solstices.[8] In all these cases, we can obtain a strong and maybe immediate sense of how a particular landscape means, how it has a history that emerges from it and determines its locality, mainly from the effects of time and the human interventions of land artists; or sometimes a narrative is envisaged for a site and takes hold there, like the "Yellow Ramp". To that extent, then, land art plays a powerful role in revealing the story of where we are. They provide us, when they are successful, with "spectacles", with things to observe in nature; this is similar to the opportunities when "nature" is observed from within designed and adjacent places (cf. "It is really about jogging a memory of nature in a city environment"[9]).

Weilacher's book that sought connections between land art and the practice of landscape architecture was extremely stimulating for its clear exposition of the narratives, different branches and elements of land art, and for how it might teach landscape architects that "nature" is the "material of art" (p.14); thus he drew specific attention to the role of stones, wood, snow and ice, and also to the out-of-the way places, deserts and forests, which land artists have chosen for their work (beyond the reach of the commercial art world, yet not immune to the exploitation of their photographs by art galleries!). He also invoked a set of archetypal forms – lines, circles, and pyramid – all of which are built forms having a historical hinterland.

---

5 *The Writings of Robert Smithson*, pp.85–6.
6 The last two examples are the work of Andy Goldsworthy in the Grizedale Forest, Cumbria, and at Storm King in New York State.
7 Cited in Weilacher, p.23.
8 Ibid, pp.178–83.
9 See Weilacher, *In Gardens*, pp.18 (the quotation is by Thomas Balsley), 174 and 294, where this "spectacle" is announced.

The interviews with twelve designers (plus one essay on Isamu Noguchi who had died in 1988) that followed Weilacher's own discussions of land artistry are equally probing, yet there is some disconnect between the varied work of land artists and what landscape architects usually do; most of the interviewed designers found themselves only slightly connected with land art, even though Weilacher argued that land art could have provided what late 20th-century landscape architects had largely lacked, a stimulus for their expressive force[10]; but that specific stimulus was not much touted among the designers – rather they highlighted inspiration from painting or pop art (Lassus, Walker or Schwartz), concrete poetry (Finlay), sculpture (Noguchi), social concerns and community relations (Andersson), the appeal of derelict or toxic land (Latz) or of large urban or landscape forms (Karavan, Geuze), even the inspired training in their own landscape discipline (Kienast above all). There would have been more scope for exploring the "between" of landscape architecture and land art if the work of, say, George Hargreaves had been more established by 1999: a comparison between Michael Heizer's "Effigy Tumuli (Water Strider)" in Buffalo Rock State Park, Ottawa, Illinois, and such designs as Hargreaves's for Parque do Tejo e Trancão, Portugal, the landscape of Clinton Presidential Center Park (see Figure 6.3), or the Bridgewater Mitigation Area, in Washington State, would suggest the inspiration that at least one landscape architect seems to have derived from land art.[11]

Almost all the designers interviewed had made places for habitation: hotel gardens, clinics, museum gardens and even cemeteries (a final habitation of sorts), all of which *may* attend to some historical meaning or vestige, *may* allude to a local topography, or invoke familiar garden forms and obsessions. Even Hannsjörg Voth's dramatic "Himmelstreppe" ("Sky Stairway") in the Moroccan desert in the 1980s is a structure in which the artist lived from time to time; his nearby Goldene Spirale ("Golden Spiral" of 1994) is a well, an essential form of survival for nomadic tribes, which clearly references historical culture. Constructing a huge wooden chair in the midst of the Forest of Dean (Figure 7.2) might suggest ironically that a race of giants once sat there and lived on earth where pigmies now dwell. But filling a museum gallery in Munich with 50 cubic metres of earth, drilling a 30 centimetre hole into the earth for 1,000 metres, or Voth's "Reise ins Meer" ("Journey to the Sea" of a huge Egyptian mummy casket) – however exhilarating – are not places where we could live.[12] Some designs discussed by Weilacher and even those that emerged out of land art were specifically for gardens, parks and landscapes, while others were contrived for garden festivals or art exhibitions: the 1,000-metre hole was executed in the city of Kassel during the documenta VI (1977), the 1993

---

10 *Between Landscape Architecture and Land Art,* p.39. It seems to me rather that designers who found themselves interviewed in the context of a book on that topic found it hard to be drawn into its (vary varied) scope, and this elicited a rather minimal enthusiasm.

11 Cf. Weilacher, p.29, with *Landscape Alchemy,* pp.33, 113–17, and 129.

12 Respectively, Walter de Maria (cited Weilacher, pp.14 and 16), or Voth (illustrated ibid, p.64).

FIGURE 7.2 Magdalena Jetelová, Big Chair, 1985–86, Forest of Dean, Gloucestershire, UK. (Photo: Emily T. Cooperman).

"Treppe noch oben" ("Steps leading up") by Bruni & Barbarit for the European Biennial for Land Art, Object Art and Multimedia was in a disused open cast coal mine.

In the last 20 years these garden festivals have enjoyed a remarkable success, notably those at the Jardins de Métis in Canada (from 2000), at Chaumont-sur-Loire in France (from 1992), and in the many biennials and shows across Europe that are indicated by the work discussed by Weilacher, including in his own later book *In Gardens*, and by Richardson's *Avant Gardeners*.[13] These exhibitions are also – like many examples of land art – inventive and striking, and doubtless offer a more promising stimulus to landscape architects, for the good reason that these (usually temporary) exhibits allow designers to play with ideas that they might not get to do (or be allowed to do) in public places or even in private residences (where clients may exert their own authority). Indeed, given the names of those who have contributed to these festivals, it is clear that there is a more engaged play between

---

13 To these we might add Michael Kasiske and Thies Schröder, *Gardenkunst 2001 / Garden Art 2001* (Berlin: Birkhäuser, 2001) which looked, mostly, at far more practical and workaday (less avant-gardenist) materials for the Potsdam Horticultural Show.

garden makers and professional architects than was apparent thirty years ago.[14] And one idea they certainly could entertain – ironically, given that sites were temporary, and possibly appropriately – is how to make sense of where they are, its locations, its materials and cultural associations of that particular place.

The 2011 Xi'an International Horticultural Exposition in north-east Beijing was a typical if somewhat extravagant affair. A former clay quarry was remodelled into a "simulacrum of the ancient Guangyun Lake", therefore itself a re-invented historical ground; along its shorelines were established the different garden exhibits.[15] One set of these were designed by professionals ("Masters' Gardens") and another by universities ("University Gardens"), and they were all, obviously, invented for that site and not designed to be there permanently. None were gardens intended for visitors to inhabit (so in that respect, like Land Art). All were in some respects a means (in the words of Paul Ricoeur) "to become modern and return to the sources, how to revive an old dormant civilization and take part in a universal civilization". Hence both Masters' and University Gardens played with ancient garden forms and different, mythical experiences – labyrinths, forests, *horti conclusi*, cloisters, mountains, gardens of mud, mist, scent or touch, and a few that mimicked regional landscapes (Argentina, China itself). There was a Maze Garden by Martha Schwartz, WEST 8 offered a Garden of Bridges from which visitors descended under a canopy of trees, a Botanist's Garden by Gross.Max, a garden of scents from the University of Toronto (Figure 7.3); Feng Chia University offered an Eco-Time garden and Columbia University offered an Eco-Plane one. This last, like many of these small enclosures, where there was limited scope for extended narratives, played with the very surface of their sites, in Columbia's case a "sliding deck" or shifting *plane* for the feet of visitors; paths and routes (the tapering courtyards of Schwartz's Maze, the bottomless hole by Topotek 1) played a fundamental role in registering the ground, as Karl Kullman's own diagram of the layout of the different gardens suggests (Figure 7.4). All were contained in garden "rooms", a feature inevitably of other sites with limited space,[16] and in the Masters' Gardens each room was protected with bamboo screens; the University Gardens had no such buffer, and were open on all sides to other gardens or to the lake.

The references were variously designed to involve visitors in negotiating the labyrinths or forests, and following routes, some of which were deliberately

---

14 I take up this aspect of place-making in a forthcoming book on *The Making of Place: Modern and Contemporary Gardens*, to be published by Reaktion Books. In her introduction to *Hybrids* (see below, footnote 17) Lesley Johnstone notes that gardens need to recover a special place now within the professional world of landscape architecture.

15 I am indebted to the discussion and analysis by Karl Kullmann, "De/framed visions: Reading two collections of gardens at the Xi'an International Horticultural Exposition", *Studies in the History of Gardens and Designed Landscapes*, 32/3, pp.182–200, where the site, garden layouts and images are presented. I quote his remarks and that by Paul Ricoeur, from *History and Truth* (Evanston, IL: Northwestern University Press, 1961), p.277.

16 The 2000 Summer Festival at Métis was dedicated specifically to garden rooms, see *Chambres Vertes* (Montréal: Bibliothèque nationale du Québec, 2001).

FIGURE 7.3 The Scent Garden, by the University of Toronto, Xi'an International Horticultural Exposition, China, 2011 (Photo: Karl Kullmann).

confusing ("forking paths", by now an old Borges *topos*), responding to sensory stimuli, and perhaps registering myths that have been associated with national gardens or cultural landscapes; but they did not seem particularly concerned to promote historical meanings *per se* in either the gardens or, inevitably, on the site itself. If they achieved anything it was to identify or construct an invented or factitious place, temporary and spatially limited (obviously) and therefore highly concentrated and usually metaphoric or symbolic. As Kullmann has suggested, it is really only when a garden is explained (by a designer, or by a visitor like himself), or perhaps is given a name that initiates our thinking, that these rather gnomic projects make much sense; that is true above all when festival designs are accompanied by texts, as in the volume *Hybrids* (les Jardins de Métis), or as when there are guided tours to Les Jardins d'Imagination.[17]

Such gardens as were exhibited at Beijing Exposition are often the occasion for what Tim Richardson calls "conceptual gardens" (the French term "concepteur" is more apt here as it privileges the maker of them). If Weilacher saw land art as a stimulus to landscape architects, Richardson obviously sees the same opportunity

17 *Hybrids: Reshaping the Contemporary Garden in Métis,* ed. Lesley Johnstone (Vancouver: Blueimprint, 2007). On the Gustafson garden, Hervé Brunon and Monique Mosser, *Le jardin contemporain: Renouveau, expériences et enjeux* (Paris: Nouvelles Editions Scala, 2011), where they note that this garden is encountered only on guided tours, and they add how regrettable it is that a visitor cannot "déambuler à leur guise et se livrer aux rêveries d'une promenade solitaire" (p. 62).

Land art and garden festivals **145**

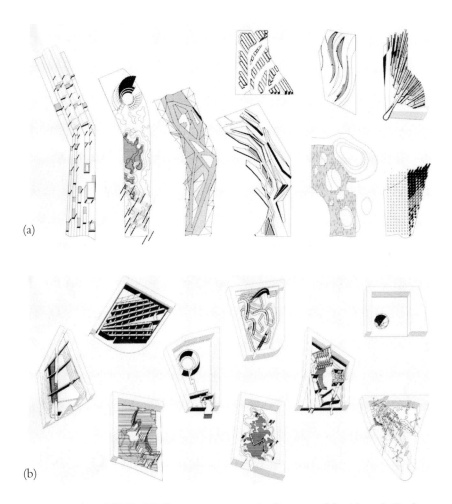

FIGURE 7.4 (a and b) Karl Kullmann, axonometric diagrams of the Master's Gardens and the University Gardens at the Xi'an International Horticultural Exposition, China, 2011. (Courtesy of Karl Kullmann).

in garden festivals, to which he frequently points. The sites and images collected in *Avant Gardeners* are endlessly intriguing, provoking and sometimes suggestive of what larger and more public, urban spaces could be. Richardson's range of reference is impressive, as are his confidence in both his own taste and his identification of conceptualism. His enthusiasm for colour in designs and for a clear evidence of humour sustain many of his examples. But many invented histories are not particularly, if at all, conceptual, unless what is meant is simply to signal how a scheme is over-reliant upon one idea (if that is what he means by "meaning", another of his key conceptualist terms, but one that applies equally to the Villa

146 Land art and garden festivals

Lante or Versailles). Two elements of his argument, however, seem problematical: one concerns the role of history, already discussed in the previous chapter, the other is whether conceptualists provide places as opposed to concepts. We are once again into the issue of inhabitation.

Richardson comments that landscape and garden exhibits at Métis "brought out the best and worst in designers" (though that doesn't apply only to festival exhibitors but to all designers!).[18] But it does direct attention to his theme of conceptualism. His several pages of aphorisms ("Maxims Towards a Conceptualist Attitude" (pp.232–40) ask for "mind gardening", as well as alpine gardening, vegetable gardening and other activities we already know about. Now the artist, Carl André, objected to conceptualists by saying that "an idea in the head is not a work of art ... A work of art is out in the world, is a tangible reality".[19] It recalls (improbably and maybe improperly) the aphorism by Thomas Hobbes that "the masse of all things that are is Corporeal ... every part of the Universe, is Body, and that which is not Body, is no part of the Universe".[20] The point is well taken, and in landscape architecture an idea best needs to be "brought to presence" (Georges Descombes' formulation used earlier), even if the visitor may find that what is "present" bears little relations to the "idea" conceived by the artist/designer.

The role of the artist is paramount in conceptualist gardens, and if there is any coherence to the notion of conceptual landscape design it would foreground meaning, a term that Richardson pushes to the fore in his essay on "History". He quotes Martha Schwartz that landscapes "can be about anything" and that "anything may take a variety of *forms* [my italics], including the idea of site" (i.e. "genius loci"), or some concern with history. He himself would claim (although a seeming paradox) that conceptual landscape designers are "obsessed with history".[21] While these garden festivals that he discusses are exciting, able to provoke re-thinking about how to augment the traditional vocabulary of garden-making, their sense of historical ground is limited largely because the ground itself, allotted to each designer, is impermanent (each lasting probably no more than two seasons). At most, the history that is addressed directly, or usually by implication, is the tradition and idea of the garden itself. This is the moving force behind garden festivals, examining and extending the history of gardens, escaping the merely naturalistic, the banally pastoral or the well-meaning ecological, and instead embracing abstraction and symbolism, along with new materials on their site.

---

18 This is echoed in a rather acerbic review of the Westonbirt International Festival of Gardens in 2002 by Robin Lane Fox, headlined as "Great Idea, Pity about the Results"; see *Financial Times* (14 September, 2002), p.13 in Weekend Section.

19 Quoted in *The Guardian Weekly* (15 February, 2013), p.40. André noted that he was himself "a hopeless drawer – and a terrible painter".

20 I am grateful to Michael Leslie for drawing this to my attention, although its insertion into a discussion of conceptualist gardening is of course at odds with it. From the English (1651) edition, Chapter 46, "Of Darkness from Vain Philosophy and Fabulous Traditions".

21 *Avant Gardeners*, pp.98, 33 and 97 respectively.

Land art and garden festivals 147

Richardson pits conceptualism against "the ecological attitude", and he does so by arguing that the ecologists would "create some kind of wilderness fantasy" and not "take inspiration from history" (p.145); conceptualism is "more demanding and commercially more daring than an 'ecological' sensibility" (p.146). This caricature of the ecologist may be fun for the conceptualist, but is flawed internally by its own illustration of the High Line by Field Operations: aside from strange inaccuracies of it being a "meandering" boardwalk or a "glorified wasteland", the design is hardly "entirely from nature". Its careful *abstraction* of a derelict railway, complete with fragments of new concrete rails and the quite untypical planting and corten steel edges (nothing so elegant would be found on an abandoned track), may perhaps in the design proposal have originally acknowledged ecological principles, but the built work is marked arguably by "a conceptualist aesthetic" (a phrase that Richardson applies elsewhere to Michael Van Valkenburgh[22]). The High Line is surely "artificial" and therefore "true to itself", as are other conceptualist *desiderata*, including its experimental approach (much more so than the High Line's presumed model in Paris, the Promenade Plantée), a clear sense of "meaning" focused on one idea and not simply an agglomeration of materials, hence its highlighting of the history of the former rail line into the meat packing district of New York; there is also its ability to "nourish" visitors with its "plot", its "speaking" to them of what once was there, and it is "fun" (though without recourse to plastic toys), and, above all, it is very much a "political act". The High Line may have become so crowded and over-visited that it is more a spectacle than a place to "inhabit" for a while, but it is a real place and not just one that simply parades attitudes or concepts, as in some garden exhibit. It surely has been "brought to presence".

Certainly, Smithson's claim that art degenerates as it approaches gardening, is not remotely apt when so many exhibits take up the idea of the garden. Both exhibitors' own manifestos and visitor responses are what chart the role of the garden's place within its own history, and almost every exhibit seems to narrate the process of its own design[23] and sometimes the relation of the site to the immediate or larger landscape. At Métis the gardens could look inwards – rooms for inhabitation, if a touch facetiously, and for play and gardening activity itself; and outwards to the shoreline of the St Lawrence River, either by incorporating representations of that landscape (tidal flats, salt marshes) into a specific garden, or (responding to the spell of land art) colonizing a tiny island in the River, where two pillars of salt, slowing disintegrating, amid the debris of a cormorant's nesting ground, could be glimpsed through binoculars on land.

22 Ibid, p.146. What follows are items taken from Richardson's "Maxims Towards a Conceptualist Attitude to Landscape Design". When he quotes as one of his maxims, "A garden can be a retreat. Or it can be a strategic withdrawal. It might equally be an attack", it bears an uncanny and unacknowledged debt to Finlay's "Certain gardens are described as retreats when they are really attacks", except Finlay's aphorism is sharper and more gnomic, Finlay being after all (what he himself professed) a poet, a Scots "Maker".

23 See remark by Bernard St. Denis in the foreword to *Hybrids,* p.7.

148 Land art and garden festivals

While "gardeners are innately conservative", as the Métis director, Alexander Reford notes, it requires some "act of daring" to go past the conventional notion that gardens were simply about plants and less about design. Yet in the restricted spaces of exhibition plots, design is necessarily predominate, nor is a *"lack* of daring" very apparent! And many exhibits were, nonetheless, wonderfully *about* plants, presenting them in ways that were unusual – in pots stacked on the grass as if "they had been delivered off a ship", or where stainless steel panels or bands mirrored surrounding plants, reflecting in their slices of metal a jungle of castor plants or ferns from Québécois forests (Figure 7.5); or simply by insisting that "a garden [be] made with plants by a designer concerned with knowing and revealing complexity", accompanied by a garden of squares alternating panels of water with meconopsis plants reflected in them.[24]

Reford also argues that the Métis Festival places itself within the "evolving practice of landscape architecture" with a focus on climate change, recycling, forest

FIGURE 7.5 Philippe Coignet and David Serero, "Modulations", project for Les Jardins de Métis in 2005. Shiny steel screens, themselves derived from growth patterns in the plants, reflected the leaves of ferns, their reflection "cast the boundaries of the garden back into the space itself". (Photo courtesy of Louise Tanguay).

24 Ibid, pp.40, 52–5 and 120. See also *Avant Gardeners*, p.222, though here too symbolism (blue flowers signalling hope and reconciliation), a Genette-like quotation from Raymond Queneau's *Les fleurs bleues,* and meconopsis being a "signature flower" at Métis, are all convened to extend the meaning of this garden.

management and genetically modified plants.[25] Several gardens were laboratories, literally, or satirically: so for Paul Cooper's The Eden Laboratory (plexiglass boxes to declare how humans have lengthened seasonal growth or how coloured lights affect plants – "A virtual torture chamber for plants"); in the "Core Sample" garden were plants in narrow glass test tubes, and genetic experiments, were displayed in the confrontational and unexpected "In Vitro" exhibit by NIP Paysage. Garden materials, for themselves or symbolically, were also part of the extended laboratory – the asphalt, plastic colours, strange shapes, Blue Sticks as an alternative version of some herbaceous border of blue flowers – everything you'd ever wanted, or possibly not, in a landscape of your own. "Not in My Backyard", by espace dur, perhaps satirically, made visitors aware that even in their backyard panels of turf on top of exposed wire mesh were not implausible.[26]

The impact of these festivals is exciting and even discomforting; they evince humour and can "affront" the visitor (Reford's word). Such responses in themselves are perhaps sufficient to justify these events. But beyond these exhibitions is the question of how these ideas will permeate the professional, and explicitly the public, domain. Established landscape architects have enormous fun on these occasions, as the published imagery of their exhibits also makes clear. The firm Land-I ('I for Italy') has had installations at Chaumont-sur-Loire, Métis and Westonbirt in Gloucestershire, and seeks to identify "historical nuances" in different places and occasions. At Westonbirt, stacks of wooden crates contained plants from every continent, all carefully labelled, which spoke to the fashion, if not the frenzy, of historical plant collection and importation. The "Daisy Garden", also at Westonbirt by Die Landschafts Architekten, where the children's game of pulling petals from a daisy ("He loves me, he loves me not…"), was played in an enclosed space of love seats.[27]

But sometimes festivals or temporary designs suggest a more sustained look at how larger and more permanent landscapes could be envisaged. Thus the High Line, while not emanating from such events (Field Operations have never chosen to exhibit in them), makes clear how such quasi-conceptualist design can have a huge public resonance. So, too, the installation by Kathryn Gustafson and Neil Porter for the Venice Biennale of 2008, which was a temporary insertion within a disused segment of the Arsenal; this is a famed, if largely derelict, ground of some historical importance in the narrative of the Venetian Republic. And one of the design's elements also opted to install a vegetable garden where an earlier one had existed in a former nunnery nearby. But the invention largely yielded a truth bigger than these fragmented pasts.

---

25 Quoted in ibid. Other publications also claim that garden festivals or exhibitions can stimulate professional designers, like the subtitle of *Badlands: New Horizons in Landscape*, ed. Denise Markonish (North Adams, MA: Massachusetts Museum of Contemporary Art, 2008).

26 *Avant Gardeners*, pp.82, 148–9, 152–5 and 136–7.

27 Ibid, p.167 for LAND-I, and for The Daisy Garden, pp.172–3 and 199 (the Limelight that follows later).

150 Land art and garden festivals

FIGURE 7.6 Kathryn Gustafson and Neil Porter, plan for their installation, "Towards Paradise", at the Venice Biennale, 2003. The Store Room or cabinet is connected by paths to the green lawn of Contemplation and the vegetable garden of Nourishment. (Courtesy of the designers).

The installation comprised three elements (Figure 7.6): a cabinet of curiosities, a vegetable garden, and an open, grassy area. These three together suggested a past – the cabinet; the present – the rich harvest of mature plants in the vegetable plot; and a future – the empty oval space that (at least for the opening) was graced with clouds of white cloth floating above. The richness of this event was that these three temporal zones interacted with each other: the vegetable plot was made in the spirit of earlier city gardens in Venice, but this historical allusion was compounded by having today's plants grown in advance and moved here for the presentation; the cabinet offered an assortment of extinct plants and animals, of the sort that Venetians would have collected in the past and probably displayed in a garden setting or pavilion, yet it was also a store room to be studied by present day visitors; the open grassy bank was a gesture to a modernist, uncluttered "nature", yet the clouds floating above it were reminiscent of Tiepolo's 18th-century ceilings. Furthermore, the vegetable plot, situated on the path *between* the cabinet of curiosities and the open, grassy oval, implied a historical sequence that elicited a new art out of a well-considered exploration of its various pasts. In this city, where the future is, maybe sadly, just about the past, the Gustafson and Porter design held up the possibility of a new future for gardens in a city once famed for them and their botanical expertise.[28]

The Venice garden was temporary, like most presentations in the Biennale, but this in itself marked its modernity, a temporary garden being something unusual in earlier cultures. Yet at the Westonbirt Arboretum, Meyer + Silberberg's installation did what had often been done on many estates, isolating a tree and honouring its age, its growth or extraordinary shape; thus designers *can* still invoke "a catalogue of reusable features" without being post-modernist; they can be reused, because most features are old devices (apart from asphalt, plastic, aluminium and other modern materials) and can be nonetheless presented in much festival work in both histrionic as well as historical mode. Meyer + Silberberg isolated an existing and therefore old item – a single sycamore tree. The project was entitled "Limelight" (Figure 7.7): within a sculpted declivity, the "humble" tree was surrounded with a circle of gravel around its trunk and then by rising grass banks ("an earthen medallion"), which allowed the tree to 'speak for itself' more eloquently and insistently in the limelight of its new amphitheatre than if it had been lost in the woods. Visitors could recline on the banks to watch the performance.

FIGURE 7.7 David Meyer and Ramsey Silberberg "Limelight", Westonbirt Garden Festival 2003. (Courtesy of the designers).

28 See my *The Venetian City Garden: Place, Identity, and Perception* (Berlin: Birkhäuser, 2009), specifically pp.187–8, and Raffaella Fabiani Giannetto's article "The Use of History in Landscape Architecture Nostalgia", special issue on "Nostalgia" in *Change Over Time* (Spring, 2003), pp.107–9.

152 Land art and garden festivals

A consideration of garden festivals, as equally with land artists working in remote situations, has suggested that private and the public domains have been pulled apart ever since actual public parks (not aristocratic ones that were opened occasionally) were instituted by the end of the 18th century, beginning with Munich's English Garden; though sometimes they have occasionally managed to re-negotiate that dialogue between public and private. Perhaps we actually need the rival and mutually challenging modes of professional and largely public work on the one hand and private garden designer and even amateur on the other; the two complement, clarify and critique each other's work.

Except there is evidence that an exchange, rather than a rivalry between them, is forthcoming. A collection of essays by Brunon and Mosser focus precisely on such liaisons, discussing or illustrating in their book some examples familiar by now, like the Little Sparta (their volume is dedicated to Ian Hamilton Finlay), the Garden of Cosmic Speculation, Kathryn Gustafson's Terrasson-Lavilledieu garden, Jardin Atlantique and other Parisian parks, and well as several gardens contributed to the exhibitions at Chaumont-sur-Loire. But they also, good European historians, cast their net wider to include earlier prototypes of public and private work where concepts tend to predominate and are "in play" ("*enjeux*", as in their subtitle): the work, for example, of Achille Duchêne, Gabriel Guévrékian, Isamu Noguchi, Russell Page, Cecil Pinsent, and even a section on "Écologie Concrete" (*pace* Richardson who thought conceptualists had nothing to do for or with ecology).[29] Their scope, though, manages only slight references to designers in the United States, and two names in particular there make some sense of both the useful dialogue between public work and gardens associated directly or indirectly with garden festival mentality.

Both Martha Schwartz, much championed, rightly, by Richardson, and also Ken Smith, to which I turn finally, seem to work largely in public spaces and yet involve many conceptualist "attitudes". Smith himself has contributed to various temporary installations: at Liberty Plaza in New York, for the winter solstice of 1977, he provided a Glowing Topiary Garden (with Jim Conti as lighting designer) – sixteen 16-foot cones, with a larger one in the centre of the plaza; these were illuminated by white and coloured lights, set amidst the careful quincunx of locust trees, that Smith termed "a French topiary"; but the trees themselves were set in the iron tree plates designed originally by Aphonse Alphand in the 19th century[30] – so an additional French note. Equipped, too, with wind chimes and electronic

---

29 Hervé Brunon and Monique Mosser, *Le jardin contemporain: Renouveau, expériences et enjeux* (Paris: Nouvelles Editions Scala, 2011). Some garden-like installations have appeared in established and semi-public places, like Beatrice Farrand's gardens at Dumbarton Oaks in Washington, DC, or Marks Hall in Essex, UK; and arboreta also seem to believe that some such insertions of sculpture would enliven their arboreal content, like Westonbirt (though that festival has closed) or the Morris Arboretum in Philadelphia.

30 Alphand's *Les Promenades de Paris* contains a plate in the second volume captioned as "Voie publique détails"; as a result these tree guards are employed everywhere.

Smith also installed WallFlowers at different locations, from small sites (his own bathroom) to hotel and museum facades, inside galleries, and at the Cornerstone Festival of Gardens in Sonoma, CA: on invisible grids, or on a scrim of coloured construction fencing, were randomly attached multi-coloured flowers in synthetic fabrics. No one installation was ever the same, and they provide vertical gardens of latticework clothed with artificial flowers.[31] He has also designed a whole series of vertical gardens, some in stainless steel, triangular baskets, some on stainless steel frames and expanding mesh for a "folding topiary wall", PVC flower-pots, or ceramic, off-the shelf planters.[32] So he works to make a historical ground even where none of the sort now provided previously existed. But he has also responded, with his usual mixture of real and invented insertions, to places that have a distinct and valued cultural history.

Smith's eagerness for appropriating different materials, different forms and unexpected settings or sites – the inaccessible roof of the Museum of Modern Art in New York, with its recycled lightweight materials (crushed glass, PVC and plastic) and its sense of a camouflaged roof (though surely with a sly gesture to some paintings in the galleries below, Arp for instance) – are being extended into more conventional sites (at least on the face of it). For if his early work was designed to respond with wit and even irony to the long traditions of garden-making, his latest work tackles residual historical values of sites in Santa Fe, Mexico, or Orange Country Great Park, in Irvine, CA. Yet his eye for these larger spaces is still acute: for the Santa Fe Railyard Park (Figure 7.8), in collaboration with Mary Miss and Frederic Schwartz, he invoked gabion walls, rust-coloured concrete terracing, but also a surviving irrigation ditch, cottonwood trees, and lessons in agriculture and water conservation for kids. If Santa Fe does resemble a more conventional park, though coloured by an instinctive sense of its local history and materials, his work for Irvine on a disused airforce base will be much more startling. The former runway of the airport in Irvine will be maintained, set at a conspicuous angle through the parkland, a buried stream is revived; for Californians who either always drive or who work on hard physical jobs there will pedestrian opportunities and passive recreation; a confection of cultural venues and different micro-climates, and – a supremely Californian gesture – an invented 2.5-mile canyon, replete with palm trees and green plants: this may be "rooted in natural archetypes" (Genette-like gestures), but it and other features are "entirely synthetic".

Smith, Schwartz and David Meyer did, together, invent a wonderful pleasure park in Toronto. Yorkville Park (Figure 7.9) was constructed over a subway and

---

31 See *Ken Smith Landscape Architect*, with an introduction by John Beardsley (New York: The Monacelli Press, 2009), to which I am indebted. Beardsley calls the volume a "midcareer retrospective" (p.7). The two installations discussed here are featured on pp.34–45 and 174–83.

32 Ibid, pp.74–87. For the MOMA rooftop and the two new parklands, pp.132–45, 184–201 and 202–15 (with other colleagues, ecologists, architects and artists).

FIGURE 7.8 Ken Smith, Santa Fe Railyard Park, New Mexico. (Photo courtesy of Ken Smith & Esto photography).

parking garage, thus a literal palimpsest; further its oblong compartments echo the footings of a row of terrace houses demolished for the construction of the subway below. And also, Genette-like, it references a host of typologies (park, botanical garden, cabinet) and alludes to or quotes Ontario topography. The range of plants,

FIGURE 7.9 Ken Smith, Martha Schwartz and David Meyer, Yorkville Park, Toronto.

a criss-cross of walk-ways over the "marshland", the wire curtain that freezes in winter, the large rock (transported from the countryside) all signal the immediate locality, an epitome, as it were, of Ontario. That Smith also likened the layout to a series of caskets, each containing one specimen of the complete collection, also make this a modern, urban cabinet of curiosities. An invented place that feigns a truth larger than itself.

AFTERWORD/AFTERLIFE

"… without the 'big events' of history. Oh, maybe there are a few statues, a legend, and a couple of curios, but not past – just what passed for a future"

(Robert Smithson)[1]

"in this technological era of placelessness, perhaps our greatest challenge is to build up, not destroy, our relationship to the natural and built past"

(Robert Stern)[2]

"Every history is contemporary history"

(Benedetto Croce)[3]

Georges Descombes argued that his work involved "discovering, in the process, all that I did not know". This involved "improvisation" and "speculation" about the past to propose a new "articulation" or a "shifting" of a given place, and also to recognize time's contribution to the "future potential" of place.[4] His process of "reshaping", as with the Swiss path, seemed to occupy a mid-way point between the two historical approaches outlined in Chapters Five and Six. Yet his emphasis tended, nonetheless, towards invention (as it is termed here), or an imaginative point of view of the site: "that which one would like to be present where no one expects it any more". Any landscape architect is likely to be pulled towards imaginative invention; yet design is also always subject to the circumstances and

---

1 *Collected Works*, on Passaic, p.72.
2 *Robert A.M. Stern: Houses*, ed. Peter Morris Dixon (New York: Monacelli Press, 1997), p.11.
3 *La Storia come pensiero e come azione* (1938; Rome: Laterza, 1970), p.11.
4 See above Chapter Six.

Afterword/Afterlife **157**

conditions of the work and these, as is argued here, can be determined by history, past and present.

Hence the need for what has been called "inventive analysis",[5] crucial in any recollection and implementation of historical ground. The phrase, paradoxical as it appears (analysis should be factual and perhaps critical; while invention can be complicated and imaginative), underpins the need to understand and analyse historical events, rituals, myths, associations and even materials as a prelude for re-inventing a ground. In as much as a site has some history, it contains a narrative (or a set of associations) that needs to be spelt out. Thus Philip Sheldrake, discussing "genius loci", argues that its history has to be organized "in a form that seeks coherence", but that this narrative or "fiction may be truthful in that, while not slavishly tied to the mechanical details of events, is capable of addressing something important".[6] Now Sheldrake is not and does not write as a designer or a historian, and so it is important to emphasize that literary or historical narrative, which generally has a sequential momentum, is not apt: a designed site may have a narrative that is put together or collected (collaged) by different visitors and is formed in their imaginations rather than by a route through it. Hence the usefulness of Genette's understanding of *paratextuality* in his discussion of palimpsests: a site must needs signal its awareness of how it situates itself within the taxonomic traditions of landscape design, and by allusion, quotation[7], even plagiarism, and the commentary that touches upon the site (notices, guide books, criticism), which clearly may include historical reference.

However, just to be clear, a designer is not necessarily concerned with contributing to heritage culture (unless of course called upon to do so specifically); the landscape designer is not involved with providing "authenticity" to heritage places (this is a very tricky issue and needs consideration in its own right). In this connection, Richard Weller has rightly derided the "profitable trade in feigning intimacy with local contexts. Sometimes this business of symbolizing place might encapsulate the pride and resilience of local identity, but more often than not it smacks of insecurity, ideology and asphyxiated imagination".[8] But "symbolism" is not the business of historical ground, though it may adhere in some cases. And this is where Friedrich Nietzsche's triad of various histories – monumental, antiquarian and critical – is vital: the landscape architect's "history" must be critical above all.[9]

5   A decisive instance by Bernard Lassus, *The Landscape Approach*, p.74.
6   The chapter, "A sense of place", begins his largely theological meditation, *Spaces for the Sacred: Place, Memory, and Identity* (Baltimore, MD: Johns Hopkins University Press, 2001), pp.1–15 (in the section on place and narrative). This echoes the historian in *Baudolino* who is led to believe that "little truths can be altered so that a greater truth emerges".
7   "[T]he tropes of landscape design", Joseph Disponzio, *Territories*, p.58.
8   "Between Hermeneutics and Datascapes: A critical appreciation of landscape design theory and praxis through the writings of James Corner", *Landscape Review*, 7/1 (2000), p.12.
9   I would also refer to Kenneth Frampton's insistence on the need for designers to serve "in a critical sense, the limited constituencies in which they are grounded": "Prospects for a Critical Regionalism", *Prospecta*, 20 (1983), p.148.

158 Afterword/Afterlife

History either springs from the ground itself – geologically, topographically, historically, culturally – or the designer knows enough about its location to invent a site with a plausible, but fabricated, history. This book began by assuming that there would be sites either where history was palpable, readable and useful to a new designer, or where other places did not bother with anything that pertained to the past, either locally, historically, or in the designer's arsenal of professional resources. My exploration has shown that, while not completely wrong, the distinction was too sharp (Chapters 5 and 6 already admitted to some grey areas). Many designers gesture to the idea of palimpsest or the layering of ground, where a historical element was evident. This also involved a clear dedication to the particularities of a place, to an informed sense of its locality where some historical ground could be critically addressed. Alternatively, a historical ground could be invented.

Further, many designers felt obligated to use the past (or an invented past) specifically to address the future; this is not simply a desire for later fame, a need to be installed in the galaxy of landscape architects, nor that every project necessarily attends to the future of its own development (how will the trees grow? how will a changing climate alter its forms and appearance? How will the changing political world determine places?). It is also important to accept that an impulsion from the past, whether in design format or historical associations, propels that site into its own future. Leatherbarrow's interest in topographical stories is that it gives "evidence of previous enactments, but ... also indicate[s] those that are still occurring and may unfold in future"[10]. Hence the various mottoes at the head of this Afterword: that the past is to be the starting block for future work, that history is always about "now", and that (though Smithson may be a shade too caustic) "big events" must be for designers what can "pass" for a future. And there is some irony in all this – that the past is to be the basis or site of future use and enjoyment, rather than the dustbin of invention. Christopher Girot notices a "genuine ironic genre" in places like Duisburg, where the opposites of continuing nature and redundant industry are associated; or Smithson's ironic appeal to the monuments in Passaic, where a sand box where children might play is also "a model desert", or every grain of sand a "dead metaphor that equalled timelessness.[11]

But just as designers may envisage a future life for their projects, different people will also respond and discover their own sense of a site's relations to the past, as well as envisage or even help to decide its future; they can identify historical ground even in places where it did not seem to be evident or noteworthy. History can be, then, in the eye of the beholder, or at least in his or her imagination. This is what Augustin Berque argued as an "art of milieu"[12]: the place is not just an objective, physical place, but one that we recognize as one that *has been* made and that we

---

10 *Topographical Stories* (Philadelphia, PA: University of Pennsylvania Press, 2004), p.13.
11 *Learning from Duisburg Nord,* ed. Udo Weilacher (Munich, 2010), p.29, and Robert Smithson, "A Tour of the Monuments of Passaic, New Jersey", p.74.
12 *Les raisons du paysage: de la Chine antique aux environnements de synthèse* (Paris, Hazan, 1995), pp.11–38, and see my discussion of this idea in *Greater Perfections*, pp.8–9.

ourselves investigate. And that *making* is, importantly and obviously, the work of a designer, but also of how the place is used, understood and interpreted by its visitors.

Georges Descombes, quoting Carlos Fuentes, asked that we "need to imagine the past to recall the future".[13] These essays therefore place a burden not only on the designer who finds or invents historical ground but also on the visitor or user (there is no fully acceptable term for this, nonetheless, essential person: "audience" is perhaps useful, since it attends to the need for a design to "perform"[14]). And these visitors are the ones who in great part control the future of the site. Many of the sites discussed here seem to be directed at a new afterlife, which a designer may shape but cannot wholly control. Peter Latz, who understands how landscapes are palimpsestial, sees that former and apparently "useless" layers become visually attractive and can create new spaces, where the "imagination lets the existing ones be re-interpreted and used in new ways".[15] Latz's own skill and imagination are the prime mover, for sure; but new sites exist also with a wealth of associations or meanings discovered by others. In his discussion of modern art, Robert Irwin acknowledges a "hierarchy of meanings" in art, which depend therefore upon the "determination of value [that] lies directly in the deliberations of the *experiencing individual*".[16] And this applies also to the art of landscape architecture. After a designer has identified and registered layers in a site, its life is in the hands of the site's visitors; alternatively, the visitors can play an even larger role in discovering historical ground for themselves, such was the "garden game" that Bernard Lassus asked them to play at Barbirey-sur-Ouche. A solitary tree in the memorial site in Amsterdam or another one celebrated on a mound in the Westonbirt Arboretum in England can incite associations that the tree and the site by themselves did not have, until we meditate upon the contrivance. "Ideas", Irwin also notes, "are always wedded, in some form, to previously existing practice", and both designer and user can benefit from "the gift of seeing a little more today than [they] did yesterday".

That means, of course, that the more we ponder and visit a site, the more we may learn; but it also invites us to see its future in the past. That is perhaps how an ordinary place (a *lieu*) can become a more special one (a *haut lieu*). I have argued that historical ground "performs itself", that is to say is able to present itself to others, and thus enlarge their vision of a place. Designs have to declare themselves *as* designs, or else they are seen as commons fields, lawns and waters.[17] And so with historical ground.

13 "Displacements, Canals, Rivers and Flows", *Spatial Recall: Memory in Architecture and Landscape*, ed. Marc Treib (New York: Routledge, 2009), p.121.
14 Jane Gillete says this term, "audience", is the "parlance" of landscape architects, "Can gardens mean?" *Landscape Journal*, 24/1 (2006), p.91.
15 "The idea of making time visible", *Topos,* 33 (2000), pp.97 and 99.
16 *Being and Circumstance* (San Francisco, CA and New York: The Lapis Press and The Pace Gallery, 1985), pp.15, 17 and for the two succeeding quotations 18 (my italics) and 25.
17 I refer to William Chambers' complaint that "Capability" Brown's work was indistinguishable from common fields, or Finlay's apothegm, inscribed on a bench at Little Sparta, that "Brown made water appear as Water, and lawn as Lawn".

160 Afterword/Afterlife

Nothing, as announced at the start of Chapter One, is untouched by history. And while, as was also argued, modernist landscape architecture has tended to ignore any layering of historical event, resisting everything except the formal means of their craft, these too may (if they escape the frequent renewal and overhaul of contemporary spaces[18]) acquire a patina of the past – perhaps the accretion of event and personal occupation, the sense that some otherwise anonymous place has a life that is longer than the moment when a visitor is there. Patience rewards both the design and the visitor. To give up the past would mean little instruction for our own day.

Afterword/Afterlife.1 Lawrence Halprin's Heritage Park in Fort Worth, Texas, now in need of refurbishment; the site was designed for visitors to ponder the significance of the old fort (its ground plan is inscribed on another wall) and its situation over the river then and now. The text inscribed on the wall here reads "Embrace the spirit and preserve the freedom which inspired those of vision and courage to shape our heritage".

18 The history of such sites as the Jacob Javits Plaza in New York City is a case in point: first, the space installed a steel piece by Richard Serra, *Tilted Arc*; that was removed, as people disliked its threatening effect, and then the square was filled with Martha Schwartz's curling green benches and purple pavers; this has now given way, in its latest transformation, to a project by Michael Van Valkenburgh. But these stages do not register on site, but only in the mind of an urban historian.

SELECT BIBLIOGRAPHY

Books on contemporary landscape architecture consulted for this book

Badlands: New Horizons in Landscape, Denise Markonish (ed.) (North Adams, MA: Massachusetts Museum of Contemporary Art, 2008).

Balmori, Diana, *A Landscape Manifesto*, Introduction by Michel Conan (New Haven, CT: Yale University Press, 2010).

Fieldwork: Landscape Architecture Europe, edited by the Landscape Architecture Europe Foundation (Basel, Switzerland: Birkhäuser, 2009).

Foxley, Alice, *Distance & Engagement: Walking, Thinking and Making Landscapes: Vogt Landscape Architects* (Zürich, Switzerland: Lars Müller Publishers, 2010).

Grounded: The works of Phillips Farevaag Smallenberg, Kelty McKinnon (ed.) (Vancouver, Canada: Blueimprint, 2010).

Hybrids: Reshaping the Contemporary Garden in Métis, Lesley Johnstone (ed.) (Vancouver, Canada: Blueimprint, 2005).

Intermediate Natures: The landscapes of Michel Desvigne, with a preface by James Corner (Berlin: Birkhäuser, 2009).

Kiley, Dan and Amidon, Jane, *Dan Kiley: The Complete Works of America's Master Landscape Architect* (Boston, MA: Bulfinch Press, 1999).

Landscape Alchemy: The Work of Hargreaves Associates, George Hargreaves *et al.* (eds) (San Rafael, CA: ORO Editions, 2009).

Landscape Infrastructure: Case Studies by SWA, Ying-Yu Hung *et al.* (eds) [The Infrastructural Research Initiative at SWA] (Basel, Switzerland: Birkhäuser, 2011).

Mosaics, WEST 8 (Basel, Switzerland: Birkhäuser Architecture, 2007).

Mosbach, Catherine, *Traversées/Crossings* (Paris: ICI Consultants, 2010).

Olin: Placemaking, introduction by John R. Stilgoe, and with contributions from the Olin partners in conjunction with outside authors (New York: Monacelli Press, 2008).

On Site: Landscape Architecture Europe, edited by the Landscape Architecture Europe Foundation (Basel, Switzerland: Birkhäuser, 2009).

Péna, Christine and Michel, *Pour une troisième nature/For a third nature* (Paris: ICI Consultants, 2010).

162 Select bibliography

Planetary Gardens: The Landscape Architecture of Gilles Clément, Alessandro Rocca (ed.) (Basel, Switzerland: Birkhäuser, 2007).

Reconstructing Urban Landscapes: Michael Van Valkenburgh Associates, Anita Berrizbeitia (ed.), Foreword by Paul Goldberger (New Haven, CT: Yale University Press, 2009)

Richardson, Tim, *Avant Gardeners: The Visionaries of the Contemporary Landscape*, with a Foreword by Martha Schwartz (London: Thames & Hudson, 2008).

Rinaldi, Bianca Maria, *The Chinese Garden: Garden Types for Contemporary Landscape Architecture* (Basel, Switzerland: Birkhäuser, 2011).

Shaping the American Landscape, Charles A. Birnbaum and Stephanie S. Foell (eds) (Charlottesville, VA: University of Virginia Press, 2009).

Shannon, Kelly and Smets, Marcel, *The Landscape of Contemporary Infrastructure* (Rotterdam: NAI Publishers, 2010).

Ken Smith: Landscape Architect, with Introduction by John Beardsley (New York: Monacelli Press, 2010).

Territories: Contemporary European Landscape Design, Joseph Disponzio (ed.) (Easthampton, MA: Spacemaker Press for Harvard Graduate School of Design, 2007).

Übergänge: Zeitgenössische deutsche Landschaftsarchitektur/Insight Out: Contemporary German Landscape Architecture, Stefan Lenzen *et al.* (eds) (Basel, Switzerland: Birkhäuser, 2007).

The Vanguard Landscapes and Gardens of Martha Schwartz, Tim Richardson (ed.) (London: Thames & Hudson, 2006).

Vogt, Günther, *Miniature and Panorama: Vögt Landscape Architects Projets 2000–12* (Zürich, Switzerland: Lars Müller Publishers, 2012). [This updates and extends the coverage of projects in the similarly titled book from 2006].

Waugh, Emily, *Recycling Spaces. Curating the Urban Evolution: The Work of Martha Schwartz Partners* (Novato, CA: ORO Editions, 2011)

Weilacher, Udo, *In Gardens: Profiles of Contemporary European Landscape Architecture* (Basel, Switzerland: Birkhäuser, 2005).

INDEX

Agence Ter/Henri Bava 27, 96
Alphand, Alphonse 15–16, 27, 45, 50, 153
Andersson, Sven-Ingvar 141
André, Carl 146
Angé, Marc 133
Appleton, Jay 17–18
Arad, Michael 67
Aran Isles 26
Arboreta *see also* botanical gardens
artfulrainwater web site 42

Atelier Bruel-Delmat 86
Barcelona, Parque del Clot 84, 112–14, Fig 6.5
Barragan, Luis 20, 35, Fig 2.3
Battlegrounds 70–3, 77: Waterloo 70–1;
    Gettysburg 71; Flanders Fields 71–3, Fig 5.4
Baudelaire, Charles 120, 133
Baxter, Sylvester 18–19
Beardsley, John 138 n.1, 140
Beaujour, Michel 42–3
Beirut, Lebanon, Garden of Forgivness 74–6, 134, Fig 5.5
Berger, Alan 79
Berque, Augustin 12 n.20, 158
Berrizbeitia, Anita 19,112
Blair, Tony 1
Bonnefoy, Yves 11–12, 48
Borges, Jorge Luis 144
Boston, Massacusetts 18–19
Botanical gardens 95, 99–104, Figs 5.17 and 5.18

Bürgi, Paolo (various sites) 19–22, 29, 33, 83, 108, 135–7, Figs 2.2, 2.9, 6.16 and 6.17
Burlington, Lord 12–13
Byrd, Warren 99–100

Calvino, Italo 8
Castle Howard, Yorkshire 17–18, Fig 2.1
Chatsworth, Derbyshire 18
Chaumont sur Loire (Garden Festival) 142
Coignet, Philippe 148 Fig 7.5
Coleridge, Samuel Taylor xii, 60
Corner, James (Field Operations) 79–80, 92–3, 147, 149, Fig 5.7
Cotman, John Sell 32
Cribier, Pascal 96
Croce, Benedetto 156

Danto, Arthur 117, 119
Descombes. Georges 96, 107–9, 156, 159, Fig 6.2
Desvigne, Michel 85–6
Doss, Erika 63, 66
Duchêne, Achille 152

Eckbo, Garrett 96, 97, 110 n.11
Eco, Umberto 8–9, 132
Eliot, Charles 18–19
Evelyn, John 59

Fermor, Patrick Leigh 126
Finlay, Ian Hamilton 120–5, 141, Fig 6.11;
    Little Sparta 120–5, 152, Fig 6.10;

164 Index

Fleur de l'Air 128–30, Fig 6.14
Freud, Sigmund 10, 11
Frost, Robert 1
Fuentes, Carlos 159
Fulton, Hamish 27

garden festivals 142–52, 153, Figs. 7.3, 7.4, 7.5
garden forms and elements 53–5, 56, 95–102, 104–5
Genette, Gérard 9, 24, 28, 81, 112, 124, 154, 157
Genius loci 12–14, 28,
Geology 17–27, 109, 120
Geuze, Adriaan *see* WEST 8
Gillette, Jane 119
Gilpin, William 43
Girot, Christopher 69–70, 158
Gomes da Silva, Joao 91, 92, Fig 5.14
Greenblatt, Stephen 1
Grigson, Geoffrey 22–4
Gross.Max 93–4, 97, 134, 143
Guévrékian, Gabriel 152
Gustafson, Kathryn 74–6, 125–6, 130, 134, 144, 149–51, 152, Figs 5.5, 7.6

Haag, Richard 79
Halprin, Lawrence (various sites) 4, 11, 43–4, 97, 160, Figs. 1.1 and 2.15; Afterlife/Afterword 1
Hargreaves, George (various sites) 33–5, 39–40, 41, 80 n.24, 109–12, 141, Figs 2.10, 6.3 and 6.4
Hawkstone, Shropshire 18
Heidegger, Martin 140
Heizer, Michael 25, 139, 141, Fig 7.1
Het Loo, Netherlands 6–8, Fig 1.3
Hobbes, Thomas 141
Holt, Nancy 139
Homer 112, 130
Houghton, Norfolk 7, Fig 1.2

Irwin, Robert 159

Jencks, Charles, Garden of Cosmic Speculation 117–20, 152, Figs 6.7, 6.8, 6.9
Jetelovà, Magdalena 142, Fig 7.2
Johnson, Samuel 2
Joyce, James, (*Ulysses*) 112, 133

Karavan, Dani 141
Kent, William 13, 87
Kienest, Dieter 141

Kiley, Dan 100–1, Fig 5.16
Knight, Richard Payne 12, 32
Kullmann, Karl 143–5, Fig 7.4

land art 111, 138–42, Fig 7.2
Landscape Architetcure Europe Foundation publications: *Fieldwork* and *On Site* 93–4
Lassus, Bernard (various sites) 20–1, 22–3, 88–9, 99, 106–7, 114–16, 130, 141, 159, Figs. 2.4, 2.5, 5.12, 6.1 and 66
Latz, Peter + Partner (sites and projects) 82–3, 84, 158, 159, Figs 5.9 and 5.10
Leatherbarrow, David 26, 158
Le Courbusier 116
Leviseur, Elisa 33
Libeskind, Daniel 63
Locality *see genius loci*

Macfarlane, Robert 2 n.3, 17
Manchester, Exchange Square 76–7, Fig 5.6
Maria, Walter de 111, 139
Marx, Roberto Burle 58
Memorials 63–78: Vietnam Memorial, Washington, DC 63, 68; 9/11 Memorials 67–8, Fig 5.2: Holocaust 64–6, Fig 5.1; Invalidenpark Berlin 68, 69–70, Fig 5.3; Bijlmer Memrial, Amsterdam 68–9, 159
memory systems 10–11, 119–20
Métis Gardens, Canada 142, 144, 146, 147–8, Fig 7.5 *see also* garden festivals
Meyer + Silberberg 151, 153–4, 154, 159, Fig 7.7
Meyer, Elizabeth 33
Miss, Mary 139
Moore, Henry 65
Morel, Jean-Marie 15–16, 27
Mosbach, Catherine 103
Mount Everest 2

Narrative/narratology 4, 5, 109
Netherlands, The 36–7
New York City, High Line 92–3, 135, 147; Prospect Park, Brooklyn 33; Robert F. Wagner Park, Battery City 3; Teardrop Park 24, 37, Fig 2.6
Nietzsche, Friedrich 11, 157
Noguchi, Isamu 141, 152
Nora, Pierre 64
Norway Tourist Route 95
Nostalgia 1, 11, 12, 86–8, 91, 92–2

Oldenburg, Henry 13
Olin, Laurie (and Olin Studio) 3, 42, 100, Figs 2 2.14, 5.15
Oudolf, Piet 92, 98

Page, Russell 152
Palimpsests 6–10, 45, 112
PARIS: Jardin Atlantique 5 n.7, 9, 53, 57–60, 62, 134, 152, Figs 4.4 and 4.5; Jardins d'Eole 53, 60, Fig 4.6; Desert de Retz 9, 45, 48, Fig 3.3; Parc André Citröen 53–5, 78, 96, 104, Fig 4.1; Parc Bercy 9, 53, 55–6, 61, 78, Fig 4.2; Parc des Buttes Chaument 9, 45, 50, Fig 3.4; Parc (formerly Jardin) Diderot 53, 56–7, 61–2, Fig 4.3; Parc la Villette 10; Promenade Plantée 92, 147
Parkinson, John, *Theatrum Botanicum* 98
Péna, Christine and Michel 60
Philadelphia 79–80
Pinsent, Cecil 152
Plants and planting 88–9, 95–102
Ponge, Francis 114, 116
Pope, Alexander 12–3, 14, 24, 28, 43, 129, 139
Porter, Neil 74–6, 97, 134, 149–51, Fig 7.6
Praz, Mario 35
PROAP (various sites and projects) 30–3, 39, 40–1, 71–3, Figs 2.7, 2.8, 2.13 and 5.4
Proust, Marcel 86
Provence gardens 126–30, Figs 6.12 and 6.13 *see also* Finlay, Ian Hamilton

Reed, Chris (STOSS Landscape Urbanism) 88, 89–91, Fig 5.13
Repton, Humphry 32
Resnais, Alain 5
Richardson, Tim 132–46, 147, 152
Ricoeur, Paul 143
Riffaterre, Michel 9
Robinson, William 50
Roger, Alain 12
Rome (Italy) 45–7, 54, 119, Figs 3.1 and 3.2
Rousham, Oxfordshire 13, 87
Rousseau, Jean-Jacques 124,129
Royal Society (UK) 13–14
Rudwick, Martin J.S. 19

Ruhr (Germany) 33, 82–3, Fig 2.9
Ruskin, John 30

Schjetnan, Mario 14
Schwartz, Martha 76–7, 78, 83–4, 130–2, 134, 141, 143, 146, 153, 153, Figs 5.6, 6.15 and 7.9
Sebald, W.G. 70–1
Shakespeare (*As You Like It*) 10, 126
Sheldrake, Philip 157
Silva, Joao Gomes da Fig 5.14
Smith, Ken (various sites and projects) 37, 97, 152–5, Figs 7.8 and 7.9
Smithson, Robert, 77–8, 139, 140, 147, 156
Spenser, Edmund 79
Stern, Robert 156
Stevens, Wallace 111
Stourhead 5 n.8
Stowe, Buckinghamshire 22, 43

Tati, Jacques 59
Thresholds 72, 74, 94
Tolkin, Wiktor Fig 5.1
Topography 27–35, 109
Towne, Francis 32
Tshumi, Bernard 10–11
Tunnard, Christopher 97

Van Valkenburg, Michael (various sites) 24–5, 37, 39, 81–2, 147, Figs 2.6, 2.12 and 5.8
vertical walls 139, 153 *see also* plants and planting
Vogt, Günther 26–7, 30, 33, 37–8, 89, Fig 2.11

Walker, Peter 67, 99, 141
Washington, DC, FDR Memorial 4–5, 11, Fig 1.1
Weather,16, 35–44
Weilacher, Udo 98, 125, 126, 140–1
Weller, Richard 37 n.35, 157
WEST 8 (various sites and projects) 36–7, 87, 135, 141, 143, Fig 5.11
Windsor Great Park, Berkshire 17–18

Young, James E. 64 n.1, 64–5

Taylor & Francis
eBooks
FOR LIBRARIES

ORDER YOUR FREE 30 DAY INSTITUTIONAL TRIAL TODAY!

Over 23,000 eBook titles in the Humanities, Social Sciences, STM and Law from some of the world's leading imprints.

Choose from a range of subject packages or create your own!

- Free MARC records
- COUNTER-compliant usage statistics
- Flexible purchase and pricing options

- Off-site, anytime access via Athens or referring URL
- Print or copy pages or chapters
- Full content search
- Bookmark, highlight and annotate text
- Access to thousands of pages of quality research at the click of a button

For more information, pricing enquiries or to order a free trial, contact your local online sales team.

UK and Rest of World: online.sales@tandf.co.uk
US, Canada and Latin America:
e-reference@taylorandfrancis.com

www.ebooksubscriptions.com

A flexible and dynamic resource for teaching, learning and research.